W9-CBC-854

# Blindsided by the Taliban

# Blindsided
# by the Taliban

A JOURNALIST'S STORY OF WAR, TRAUMA, LOVE, AND LOSS

## CARMEN GENTILE

Skyhorse Publishing

Skyhorse Publishing books may be purchased in bulk at special discounts for sales promotion, corporate gifts, fund-raising, or educational purposes. Special editions can also be created to specifications. For details, contact the Special Sales Department, Skyhorse Publishing, 307 West 36th Street, 11th Floor, New York, NY 10018 or info@skyhorsepublishing.com.

Skyhorse® and Skyhorse Publishing® are registered trademarks of Skyhorse Publishing, Inc.®, a Delaware corporation.

Visit our website at www.skyhorsepublishing.com.

10 9 8 7 6 5 4 3 2 1

Library of Congress Cataloging-in-Publication Data is available on file.

Cover design by Michael Wilson

Print ISBN: 978-1-5107-2968-1
Ebook ISBN: 978-1-5107-2970-4

Printed in the United States of America

For James Foley, Matthew Power,
and all the freelancers who weren't as lucky as I was.

And for all the soldiers that have ever served at Combat Outpost Pirtle King.

A portion of sales of *Blindsided by the Taliban* will go to RISC,
Reporters Instructed in Saving Colleagues. RISC teaches life-saving
first aid techniques to freelance journalists working in conflict zones.
To learn more about RISC, go to www.risctraining.org.

# CONTENTS

**PART TWO**

**PART THREE**

# PREFACE

A friend from Afghanistan was busting my balls when he said my "greatest career achievement is getting shot in the face."

I might be irked by his besmirching of the entirety of my journalistic accomplishments if he wasn't sort of right.

Sure, I've reported from dozens of countries spanning the globe, but not to great acclaim. I've never won any of the myriad awards, grants, and residencies regularly doled out to my deserving peers. In fact, I'm willing to bet few of my colleagues have ever even heard of me.

For nearly two decades I've flown under the radar, embarking on ill-conceived adventures, writing about them, and wriggling my way out of frequent personal mishaps.

It's been, for the most part, a hell of a way to make a living.

But when I got hurt something changed, both in my outward persona and inside me. Rather than being completely unknown, I became "that guy who got shot in the face in Afghanistan . . . you know, the one with the girl's name . . . what is it again?"

I made jokes about my injury when anyone would ask me to recall what happened. I've always had a penchant for dark humor, particularly as it pertains to my own predicaments. "There should've been nothing left of me," I'd say, wrapping up my umpteenth retelling of that day in Afghanistan with a wicked grin that let mouth-agape listeners know it was OK to laugh about it, too.

But I wasn't OK. I was angry, jittery all the time, and prone to sleeplessness. When I could rest, I had nightmares about being killed in every way imaginable.

When therapy and ill-conceived romantic interludes failed to ease my woes, I decided writing about what happened might help.

It didn't.

Instead, I discovered that unpacking and reexamining the worst period in my life merely amped up my cantankerousness. Even recalling the lighter moments following my injury offered no relief. Meanwhile, I drifted away from most family, friends, and loved ones with little or no explanation.

Perhaps this book offers one.

A little background on how I went about writing this book may also explain, albeit not excuse, my behavior:

I started writing *Blindsided by the Taliban* in a dilapidated cabin in Pennsylvanian Appalachia I rented during the coldest winter I can remember. In that house with its faulty furnace, rotten floorboards, and a sunken, back-aching mattress, I began cobbling together my story. I poured over hundreds of the hand-scribbled notes on napkins, assorted scraps of paper, notebooks, and my previous reporting trying to piece it all together into something resembling a coherent narrative.

After several months of writing in near-total isolation at my frosty mountain abode, the weather finally broke. I packed up my partial manuscript and notes and rode my motorcycle more than a thousand miles south to Miami. There I had a friend who said I could work at her house while she was vacationing, as long as I fed her two dogs and gave the sickly one a daily shot of insulin. Despite my extreme needle phobia, I agreed to the arrangement, injecting her poor pooch in the neck every morning before going about my business.

The change of scenery and warm weather helped me maintain my momentum, so much so that when my friend returned from her vacation I headed a little further south to a small place in the Florida Keys, where I was my most productive during the course of writing this book. But even in the tranquil, lazy Florida Keys I couldn't find peace.

By now you may be wondering how I managed to afford all this continental gallivanting, considering I hadn't done any paid work for months and freelance journalists are notoriously cash-strapped.

The answer, I'm loathe to admit, is lawyers. After years of legal wrangling with CBS over the workman's compensation they owed me from my injury, I finally received a modest settlement that allowed me to take some time off.

Amid that prolonged legal struggle, I'd imagined getting a nice stack of cash would surely make me feel better.

Again, it didn't.

Also, the settlement from CBS wasn't enough to sustain me until I completed the book. So, after a year away from the reporting game, I decided to go back to my first love and see if I could jump-start my near-dead career. In doing so, I moved to Istanbul, a popular home base for journalists covering conflict and strife. While there, my book remained my first priority—I did just enough journalism to pay the bills and remind editors I hadn't, in fact, fallen off the face of the earth during my hiatus.

I spent two years editing and polishing my manuscript and submitting it to hundreds of agents and editors, all of which said, "No thanks." I worried that my story may never see the light of day and became as despondent as when I first got hurt.

When I'd take a break from anguishing over my book to report from the Turkish/Syrian border or Iraq, I was reminded what real suffering was, something I'd inexcusably forgotten amid my obsession with my own story. The concerns of a would-be memoirist/reporter trying to find a home for his book were inconsequential compared to those who lost family, friends, and homes amid the wars. When I returned to the comfort and safety of my own home, I felt even worse than I already had for my ridiculous self-indulgence.

Only after my daughter was born did my injury angst finally subside. The demands of a newborn baby and her vulnerability were the kick in the ass I needed to pull myself out of my post–Taliban attack malaise.

And as a result, "getting shot in the face" is no longer my greatest achievement, professional or otherwise.

Knocking up my wife is now firmly atop the list, though my one-in-a-trillion injury has a tight grip on the number two slot . . . for now.

# AUTHOR'S NOTE

In a not-so-subtle homage to my beloved profession of journalism, and because I'm used to writing this way, each chapter of *Blindsided by the Taliban* has a title followed by a date and location. "Datelines," as we call them in the reporter biz.

I mention this because the story occasionally jumps back and forth in time, which is my inarticulate way of attempting to avoid the dubious descriptor of a technique known as (shudder) "flashbacks."

Now, it's been suggested to me by some publishing professionals that this narrative device is too convoluted for readers to understand. They tell me you will be hopelessly confused by a nonlinear storyline. In their estimation, you apparently possess the intellect of a Shiitake mushroom.

To that I say, "Phooey." You can handle it.

You're already familiar with this technique in movies and TV shows. Whereas they do it with bad wigs, makeup, and outdated cell phones, I use datelines.

Same thing, different technique. No biggie.

I trust you'll have no problem. Why, you've already proven your superior intellect by selecting this book. As such, a story that occasionally dips into the past will be a cakewalk.

Now kick back and enjoy.

Thanks for reading,
Carmen

# PART ONE

Autobiography is only to be trusted when it reveals something disgraceful.

—George Orwell

# CHAPTER 1
# FREELANCING IN AFGHANISTAN
SEPTEMBER 6, 2010
KUNAR PROVINCE, EASTERN AFGHANISTAN

The company commander at Combat Outpost Pirtle King only half-heartedly offers to let me tag along on a mission in the mountains that kicks off at 3:00 in the morning, probably thinking I'm not up to it. He warns me it's an all-day, ass-breaking hump up steep mountains littered with ankle-twisting rocks and Taliban boogeymen.

Though daunted by his description of the day, I tell him I'm game, convincing myself it will give me the perfect opportunity to document the difficulty of the fight in this corner of Kunar Province, a relative safe haven for militants crossing the porous border from Pakistan.

More importantly, I don't want the commander to think I'm a pussy.

I've been embedding with US forces for years, both in Afghanistan and Iraq, so I have a pretty decent idea of what it takes to get readers interested in a story. A firefight helps. So does anything blowing up, hopefully nothing that puts soldiers in harm's way. With that in mind, I insert myself into situations that will make for tantalizing reading so folks will pay attention to what's going on over here. That doesn't mean I'm not scared shitless when I do it. I just leave that part out of my stories.

I can't let soldiers see I'm scared either. It makes some of them nervous enough having a journalist in their midst, wondering whether something I'm going to report will get them chewed out by their commanders or end their careers. Worse yet would be me panicking when the action kicks off and jeopardizing their lives by doing something stupid. They can't be thinking about me when they need to focus all their attention and firepower on the guys trying to kill them.

"Count me in for tomorrow," I tell the commander as calmly as I can, hoping he doesn't notice the tremor in my right leg.

After a few hours of nervous, twilight sleep, I meet up with the men preparing in the darkness for the torturous slog ahead. During the pre-mission brief, the platoon leader warns them to keep their eyes open for snipers hiding behind the boulders and in the caves that dot the mountain. I listen to his instructions while stuffing my bag with bottles of water and nervously inhaling several knockoff Chinese Marlboro Lights. I'm up to three-quarters of a pack a day, evidenced by the mud-color phlegm I spit. That's too many for me. I wake up every morning feeling like there is a cinderblock on my chest.

My nervousness about this mission isn't unwarranted. I've had a handful of close calls on embeds in Afghanistan, most of them here in Kunar. Last summer, just a few miles south of Pirtle King, I got pinned down with a platoon along a riverbed. Gunmen tucked behind boulders and positioned on nearby hilltops fired on us from three sides. We were soundly fucked. Shots pinged off the stone and mud walls we crouched behind and it occurred to me we might not make it out. Finally we screwed up the gumption to sprint across a wide-open expanse toward a footbridge across which the armored vehicles were parked. Once across, everyone scurried for the quickest cover. A dozen soldiers piled in the back of a truck designed to hold six men. Bullets plinked off the truck's armor plating. Somehow, no one was hurt.

"Seven more days till I go home," said one soldier laughing. Pinned under 1,500 pounds of young men in the steel-walled cabin of the armored truck, I caught on camera the mass of haphazardly stacked soldiers, their faces conveying a mixture of relief and jubilation at escaping another close call in Kunar Province.

I'm preparing myself for the possibility of more of the same today at the start of our predawn excursion. We pass through the gate of the combat outpost and set out along a dirt road for a couple hundred yards, then hang a sharp right, taking a wide snaking trail upward into the side of the mountain. After ten minutes of humping up steep faces cloaked in darkness, stumbling every other step, my lungs are a raging inferno.

*Fuck, I'm thickheaded for tagging along.*

Between gasps, I tell myself for the 10,345th time that I will quit smoking as soon as I get back from Afghanistan.

*No more excuses!*

After two hours of climbing, day breaks over the jagged mountain peaks. We rest halfway up the mountain; soldiers take defensive positions while I guzzle water and try to capture the moment on video.

The sun streaks over verdant mountain faces peppered with craggy boulders and settles on the ginger-red thatch of Lt. Derek Zotto's unruly pubic hair and exposed genitalia. The inseam of his pants is ripped wide open from countless climbs in these mountains. The terrain in Kunar wreaks havoc on uniforms, blowing out crotches after just a few missions; it's a common problem for the men at Pirtle King. A few other guys are also sporting crotchless fatigues. And seeing as there's no running water at Pirtle King, Zotto isn't the only one not wearing underwear.

I conduct an impromptu, on-camera interview with Zotto on the side of the mountain in whispered tones so as not to alert any potential Taliban in our midst of our presence, urging him to keep his legs closed and try not to laugh. "It sucks never having the high ground," he muses for my video camera about the distinct disadvantage soldiers have in the mountains where Taliban fighters have the geographic advantage.

I wrap up the interview, then grab some B-roll shots of his dong, just for fun.

After our short break we slog on. Several hours later, the summit doesn't look any closer. "Are we there yet?" I ask in a coolly received effort at comic relief, knowing damn well we still have a ways to go. I groan like a child getting on his parents' last nerves while en route to Sea World.

"Ughhhhhhhh!"

I am running out of gas. My bulletproof vest and camera gear seem to be getting heavier with every step. I shouldn't bitch; my load is nothing compared to the hundred-plus pounds these guys are lugging around. Laden with extra magazines of ammo and other gear, their vests weigh twice as much as mine. Their weapons, an awkward mass of metal whose shifting weight over uneven ground constantly alters their centers of gravity, make climbing in these mountains near impossible without occasionally toppling.

Spc. Jeff Hutchins stumbles over the loose boulders and lands face forward, his legs splayed behind him. "Is my helmet crooked?" he quips in a whisper as he pops up with his Kevlar head cover cocked forward over his eyes and resting on the bridge of his nose. The rest of us suppress our laughter.

We spend the rest of the increasingly sweltering morning hauling ourselves over and around boulders until we reach our objective, a summit the soldiers dub Observation Post East. It's a flat, shadeless expanse with views of now tiny Pirtle King and the river valley below. We all shed our gear and collapse to the ground, our clothes stained with sweat that's dried into a crystallized, tie-dye pattern of salt on khaki and camouflage.

It took us eight ankle-rolling, deep-heaving hours to reach the summit. And now that we're up here, it feels like it's well over ninety degrees despite our elevation.

I look out at the terraced hillsides carved out by countless generations of Afghan farmers who still work the land with basic hand tools. I'm near passed out and dehydrated just hiking up here, and Afghans on the other side of the valley are doing it every day to tend to their vegetables. Either I'm in lousy shape or these are the hardiest people on the planet.

I dig into my bag for a drink and discover I'm down to a bottle and a half of water. Some of the soldiers are nearly dry too. My joy at reaching the top drains away and is replaced by dread of the climb down, knowing it will be a dry-throated dash back to the outpost. Meanwhile, we need to return before sunset. That's when the Taliban are more likely to attack.

After an hour's rest, Zotto orders his men to throw on their gear so we can start the long haul to Pirtle King. The descent is always quicker, but the perils are greater going down. If anyone is watching us, the climb down would be the ideal time to strike. With our heads facing down and our energy depleted, we are extremely vulnerable to potential sniper attacks from the peaks above us.

Halfway down the mountain, two soldiers suffering from severe dehydration stop dead in their tracks, their faces stark white and gaunt. Hutchins, a medic, whips out IV bags and jabs their inner forearms to pump them with fluids as they lay motionless on the mountainside. Combatting my squeamishness at the sight of the IV needles, I focus my camera on Sgt. Chris Kline, who immediately takes umbrage at the sight of my camera directed at him. "Dude, don't film this," he says, his eyes rolling back in his head due to exhaustion and extreme dehydration. His cheeks are hollow and his face the color of skim milk. A moment later he relents. "Oh, what the hell, go ahead."

This is how the war in eastern Afghanistan is fought: one long slog through the mountains after another, up and down, day after day. At least that's what I've seen in all my time here. They call them "presence patrols." It's a common tactic that strikes me as unproductive and unnecessarily dangerous. These grueling, regular humps through the mountains provide the Taliban the perfect opportunity to light up a platoon from hidden firing positions on the slopes above, making effective retaliation nearly impossible.

But I'm not a military tactician, so what the hell do I know? That said, if there's a reason for hanging soldiers' necks out for the Taliban to take clean hacks at them, I've yet to figure it out.

What little I do know of military strategy I've gleaned from the pages of history and the campaigns that make the History Channel's highlight reel— decisive wins that can change the course of the war.

But that's not how it's done in Afghanistan. There are no D-Day-like offensives with tens of thousands of soldiers going head-to-head on some predetermined battlefield to decide this thing once and for all. This isn't that kind of war. The Taliban are guerrilla fighters. Real sneaky ones, too. They play small ball. Plant an explosive here, carry out a sniper attack there. Every once in a while they'll try to overrun a combat outpost with a couple dozen guys or infiltrate the Afghan Army to take out a handful of soldiers in a surprise attack. Unlike the Viet Cong that stymied US forces in Vietnam, the Taliban aren't organized enough to attempt their own version of the Tet Offensive.

I feel like the dearth of great battles leaves young soldiers longing for a fight with historical significance. Some commanders clearly recognize this fact. However, in lieu of nationwide campaigns aimed at ending this fight once and for all, they mount smaller missions with colorful names meant to evoke strong sentiment and rally troops with sagging spirits. Operation "Eagle's Claw" or "Righteous Hammer" makes walking around the mountains with a target on your back seem like it's worth the risk. A while back on another embed, I got to sit in on a mission brief and listen to a colonel tell his junior officers how they would carry out operation "Thundercat," obviously named by one of the younger soldiers for the '80s cartoon and whose humor was lost on The Brass. Every time the colonel referred to the operation by name, a young lieutenant sitting next to me would let out a muted version of Lion-O's trademark war cry: "Hoooooooo!"

We have a problem. Sgt. Kline can no longer walk due to his dehydration. Another one of the guys broke a toe and is severely hobbled. The terrain is too steep to carry them off the mountain. Even if we could haul them down, our water situation made the extra exertion dangerous. More guys could drop out from the heat, severely diminishing their ability to retaliate in the event of an attack. With no other alternative, medevac is radioed to get the injured off the mountain. While waiting for the chopper, we sit quietly on the mountainside trying to stay low and inconspicuous. Minutes seem like hours while we bake in the afternoon sun and scan the surrounding peaks for any movement.

After about an hour of tense waiting, the steady thrumming of helicopter blades begins to echo off the mountains. Moments later, a medevac chopper hovers over us, winching a rescue paramedic to the ground because the terrain is too steep to land on. The medic fastens a harness to the injured, who are hoisted into the aircraft. Thankfully, someone in the platoon has the presence of mind to tell the medics about our precarious water situation. As the soldiers, limp with exhaustion, are hoisted into the chopper, a crew member tosses out several cases of water and Gatorade. Even before the helicopter takes off, we pounce on the drinks and gulp down several bottles, then pack as many as we can for the remainder of the march.

The soldiers resolve to get the hell off the mountain as quickly as possible. I'm struggling to keep pace as the platoon picks up the tempo hoping to beat the setting sun. By the time we are a few hundred yards from Pirtle King, we're jogging in unison as I suck deep for each breath like an asthmatic John Candy on an exercise bike.

When we stagger through the gates, I'm near hallucinating from exhaustion.

"Wait, you mean to tell me the fucking reporter made it, but two of you had to be airlifted out?" says a razzing voice as I double over to catch my breath. "I can't wait to bust their balls about that."

That I endured the rigors of what turns into a fifteen-hour excruciating slog to the top and back earns me a measure of respect with the guys. While basking in their near adulation, I try not to let them see just how wobbly I am. I find the nearest object approximating a seat and plant my exhausted ass, trying not to look too tired.

Hutchins sidles up to me. "Hey man, how old are you?" he asks. I tell him I'm 36 and fairly fit despite my incessant smoking, by my own estimation.

"Huh, you're just two years younger than my dad."

*Thanks . . . douche.*

# CHAPTER 2
# THE PIRTLE KING CLUSTERFUCK

SEPTEMBER 7, 2010
KUNAR PROVINCE, EASTERN AFGHANISTAN

Pirtle King, or PK, as everyone here calls it, is tiny. Wedged between a steep, rocky hillside and the roiling Kunar River, it is home to a company of American soldiers from the 101st Airborne out of Ft. Campbell, Kentucky. It's named for two soldiers killed in 2009 when another nearby outpost was overrun by the Taliban. They and other militant groups have a solid foothold in these parts, making it an ideal staging ground for attacks on the provincial capital, Asadabad, as well as Afghanistan's larger cities, like nearby Jalalabad and the country's capital, Kabul.

Along Kunar's shared border with Pakistan, just a couple miles from PK, there are valleys spanning the divide that are natural conduits for fighters and weapons passing with relative ease through the porous and indefensible boundary. The tough terrain, coupled with the presence of a significant number of Taliban and their supporters, is giving American military leaders fits and proving difficult for the guys on the ground.

The American troops here share PK with a small contingent of Afghan soldiers and a handful of Latvian military advisers tasked with training the Afghans. It is cramped quarters. You can sprint from one end of PK to the next in about 10 seconds. And with all the enemy fire it gets, everyone here has. The "fish in a barrel" analogy could have been invented for this place.

Mountains surround it on all sides; boulders and ravines on the slopes make for ideal cover. PK is a Taliban sniper's wet dream.

Every plywood building and sandbag-covered bunker is pockmarked with bullet holes and ragged punctures from twisted, metal fragments of rocket-propelled grenades. There might as well be a target on every rooftop. I can't for the life of me figure out why it's even here. Whoever decided to put a combat outpost in such an indefensible place (my guess: some general who's never so much as flown over the place) should be busted down to buck private and forced to tongue-clean 1,000 rancid latrines.

I'm here because I requested an embed where there would be "some action," hoping to get some good audio for CBS Radio, which is paying the freight on this assignment, and *USA Today*, one of my go-to clients for print stories, photos, and the occasional video.

The trek up the mountain didn't make for great sound, but I got some fantastic quotes and images of the hillsides carved into terraced farms that probably date back at least a couple of centuries.

I approach a young soldier with questions for the story I'm working on about the difficulties they face at PK. He regards me cautiously at first, asking me at the outset not to use his name. I sense he's not sure whether to trust me, which is understandable since I've only been here a couple of days.

When I'm embedded, some guys don't know what to make of me at first. There are those that are wary of reporters and keep their distance. They either feel they've been burned before or were briefed by their sergeants and commanders to stay away. Others eventually warm up, glad to have a new face around, someone who will listen to their stories that hasn't heard them a million times already. We talk movies I've seen and they obviously haven't and what other parts of Afghanistan are like; if it's their first deployment to the country, their particular area of operation is all they typically know. Sometimes the conversation runs deeper. They speak of loved ones back home; their kids growing up without them; domestic troubles that brew when you're gone for a year or more; wives and girlfriends that left them; alimony and child support payments they can barely afford.

But more than anything we talk sports. Everyone's got a team. Mine is the Steelers, which unless you're also an NFL fan from Pittsburgh, you probably hate with every fiber of your being due to their Super Bowls and the indefensible, boozy arrogance of their fan base.

After we gab for a while about the season that's just started, the young soldier opens up with his opinions about their predicament at PK. "When the Taliban are looking down at us, they can see everything," he says, an estimation I can confirm firsthand, having spent the previous day on the same mountain frequented by snipers. Every time I took a breather and looked down into the valley, PK was completely exposed to Taliban lurking in the slopes surrounding the base. Picking soldiers off from the mountains surrounding PK would seem fairly easy shooting for an accomplished Taliban marksman. Fortunately, that hasn't happened so far. The attacks on PK commonly come from farther away, the next valley over. Taliban launch mortars at the combat outpost, blindly hoping to land a lucky shot, or fire AK-47 rounds from the slopes overlooking it, then scatter. During our hump into the mountain, one of the guys found an unexploded, rusty mortar. Spc. Nikolai Wyckoff picked it up and blew the dust off the head and laughed. "Looks like they were trying to hit PK and just failed miserably." I took a step back before turning my camera on it to film him, as if an extra three feet would protect me from the blast were it to go off.

While the Taliban can sure as hell see them, the soldiers have difficulty spotting the militants hidden in the mountains. It's a common problem for US forces in eastern Afghanistan, but at PK it's especially difficult. The surrounding hills offer so many places for Taliban to hide and little recourse for soldiers on base other than to launch mortars into the hillside in the general direction of the attack. They may spot the occasional muzzle flash from an AK-47. If it's only a few shots, they'll fire back with mortars till the shooting stops. In the event of a complex attack featuring mortars, recoilless rounds, and other artillery, they may call in an airstrike. That is, if air assets are available. Even a sizable ordinance like a JDAM (that's Joint Direct Actual Munition, fancy speak for a big bomb dropped out of warplanes) has little effect because there are so many places to hide and survive even the largest bombardment, and the mountain appears no worse for wear. I've seen fighter jets drop what seems to be a Pearl Harbor's worth of explosives on a distant mountaintop, but after the brush fires die down and the smoke clears, it's difficult to discern with the naked eye that anything happened there. "The problem with Afghanistan is it looks exactly the same after you bomb it as it did before you bombed it" is a common expression here. That saying usually refers to the ruins of the capital amid the civil war after the Soviets left, but the same applies up here.

The soldier I'm interviewing about the challenges of fighting such an elusive enemy seems to be searching for the most diplomatic way to express just how disadvantaged they are here. It's not easy to be objective when you're constantly being targeted by an unseen enemy. "When they are looking down at us, they can see everything. But trying to see them is like trying to look through a keyhole from across the room."

*Oh, that's a money quote.*

I mark it with asterisks in my notebook so I'll remember to use it to lock off the end of the piece I'm writing.

In addition to being a favorite target for the Taliban, PK is a colossal shithole of epic proportions stuffed in a tiny package. Small combat outposts like this are poorly supplied due to the dangers of getting convoys down narrow dirt roads where planting an IED is as easy as digging out a few shovelfuls of dirt and laying in some explosives with a command wire running fifty yards up the adjacent hillside. There, the trigger man hides behind a boulder to blow up a long-awaited, much-needed truckload of water, toilet paper, bacon, or whatever necessities and desirables to high heaven.

Dangerous living and few amenities are the norm for the soldiers who see combat in Afghanistan. But this place is particularly bad, one of the worst I've ever seen. The showers and clothes washers at PK gave out long ago; consequently, no one has had a proper wash in months. Everyone reeks of mud-caked, sweat-soaked uniforms and moldering, unwashed feet. The stench would make most anyone retch. Being something of a slob, I'm usually quite at ease with filth. But this place is fucking gross even by my exceptionally lax standards. The smaller bases on nearby mountaintops have even fewer amenities, though aren't nearly as foul. They typically house a smaller number of soldiers and have the advantage of steady mountain breezes to whisk away the putrid stench. But not PK. Here, soldiers are stacked in cramped bunker-style barracks, like a long-expired tin of sardines. Their gear and uniforms reek like fine cheeses aging in a dank cave.

I make a feeble effort to clean up a bit by giving myself a baby-wipe bath. I bought a bunch before I got there and handed them out. The PX (the military's answer to Walmart, where you can buy most anything: from soap to socks, cigarettes to an Xbox) at larger bases stock up on the sanitized wipes meant for use on pink newborn behinds. Soldiers in rural hinterlands use them so they can at least feign cleanliness until they take their next shower, which for these guys might not be for a very long time. A single swipe across my brow and the moisturized toilette is a poop-brown mixture of grime and sweat. Some of the guys at PK appear to have given up even trying to get clean. They're dusty, flesh-and-bone incarnations of my favorite *Peanuts* character, Pig Pen.

Despite the unsanitary conditions and dangers of living in PK, the guys here have developed a strange affinity for the place that defies common logic. One of them attempts to explain it to me in terms that I can't use in any of the mainstream outlets for which I work. I write it down anyway.

"It's kinda like a fat chick that you don't wanna say anything about, but when someone runs their mouth you're like, 'Wait, that's my fat chick!'"


Before reviewing my photos and video from yesterday's mission in the mountains, I need to check my email. There might not be any hot water for showers here, but the Internet works. Without the latter, this place couldn't function. The military runs on its wireless communications. From orders down the chain of command to supply requests from here to headquarters, it's the one thing the army can't do without anymore. A young IT specialist once put it to me this way: "Take away every armored vehicle and other means of transport for a day and we could still fight this war, but cut off the Internet and we'd be helpless."

I need to get online to see if I have a new message from my fiancée. We're currently conducting a particularly heated back-and-forth online argument and the barbs are flying. I'm expecting her next salvo to be a doozy. Soldiers aren't the only ones whose relationships can suffer from spending too much time in Afghanistan.

Her latest criticism of me is that I shouldn't even be here. According to her, embedded journalists interfere with the mission and endanger the lives of soldiers. This opinion comes courtesy of her colleagues at the US Department of State's Bureau of Diplomatic Security, where she is a new member of Secretary of State Hillary Clinton's security detail. Her work was one of the first things that drew me to her. Now it's driving a wedge between us. Several of her male colleagues are former military and take pains to express their disdain for the media, opinions that have recently manifested themselves in several of our arguments.

"Don't you think you are getting in the way when you're with them?" she said to me a month ago, right before I left. I tell her I think it's important that people know what's happening and see the dangers military men and women face.

"Not so important that you get someone killed," she retorts without reference to, let alone expressed concern for, my safety. I don't read much into it at the time, considering her oft-professed dislike for my line of work. But since I've been in Afghanistan it's really been irking me.

*Who is she to rag on my job?*

I love journalism, though judging by my bank account it's an unrequited love. Still, I can't imagine doing anything else. I don't even consider what I do "work"—it's more a cross between compulsion and a calling, with an unhealthy smattering of addiction and chronic delusion sprinkled on top.

The reporting life has afforded me the opportunity to see and do things most people can barely fathom. When I was based in Brazil, the beaches of Ipanema, where I used to surf every day, were my backyard. I climbed mountains in Bolivia on a whim after reporting on some growing unrest there. I happened across a mountaineer outfitter while in La Paz, signed on with a guide and a few days later, voilà, I'm summiting a 19,000ft. peak. "Poor in Wallet, Rich in Experience" should be carved on my headstone.

And as for embeds, I maintain it's important that folks back home know what's happening over here from the viewpoint of the youngsters risking their necks while the rest of America sits at home either Monday morning quarterbacking every perceived setback or tuning the war out completely.

I scroll through our email thread to reread where we left off in our argument, searching for tidbits that help me make my point. I've yet to answer her recent accusation that I'm too lazy to do anything about the trail of ants frequently seen scaling a wall in our bedroom. They don't bother me. I actually find their industriousness inspiring, especially when I'm lying in bed with a story deadline looming. I decide to opt out of defending my deference to the ants.

*You're not going to win this battle. Don't bother.*

Instead of crafting an email in defense of my ant fancy, I decide to pour over previous emails dating back to the beginning of our relationship, that period when we were nauseatingly in love. It wasn't all that long ago. We first got together just weeks before I left for a long stint in Afghanistan back in the fall of 2009. Seems so long ago, though it's been less than a year.

*So much has happened since then.*

I wish we could go back to those days. Maybe we could if we just stopped bickering. We tried counseling. It didn't help. Maybe we just need to decide to be happy and treat each other right.

*Could it be that simple?*

I refresh my email amid daydreams about rekindling our misplaced romance.

*Maybe she feels the same way . . .*

But there's still no response to my last message to her. It's been two days since I sent it.

# CHAPTER 3
# THANKS, CLAUDE PEPPER

MARCH 15, 2009
MIAMI, FLORIDA

For all my professed contempt for anything approximating authority, particularly the federal government, I like hanging out here.

The Claude Pepper building is named for an old Florida lawmaker whose sourpuss, oil-painted visage graces the lobby. It is a Cold War–era filing cabinet with well-worn carpets and the pervasive smell of musty bureaucracy, like an old library card catalogue that's been opened after decades of disuse.

It's just down the street from the federal courthouse where I cover the odd trial for the *New York Times* and other papers. Florida's well-deserved reputation for attracting the disreputable from around the globe doesn't disappoint. A couple months ago I saw Chuckie Taylor, the son of the former Liberian dictator Charles Taylor, get sentenced to nearly a century behind bars for assorted war crimes. Witnesses at the trial said Chuckie ate some of his victims' hearts.

When I'm at the courthouse I often pop in the Claude Pepper to see my friend Brian, who's a correspondent for Voice of America, the federally funded news agency that's also a Cold War relic. He and I sometimes work on the same stories and occasionally collaborate, though I am much more reliant on him and his superior Spanish skills than he on me. I do like to think I pull my weight by keeping him entertained when I'm over here.

"I'm going to take a wazz, then we'll go to lunch," I tell Brian on my way to the bathroom. We decided on the Italian joint around the corner.

I'm thinking it feels like a seafood linguine kind of day as I exit the bathroom and see her walking down the hall. We lock eyes and maintain our gaze while passing, stutter step, then turn to check each other out. We've both been caught blatantly body-scanning each other, then exchange awkward hellos.

"Do you work here?" she asks me in a tone that's both personal curiosity and professionally interrogatory.

"No, I hang out in the VOA office once in a while. My friend's the bureau chief," I tell her, pointing to the other end of the hallway.

I already have a vague idea of what she does, this attractive woman with a slender frame and pillowy lips. I saw her exit the offices of Diplomatic Security, a federal agency that guards diplomats, as the name clearly implies, and does some kind of investigatory stuff. I've seen the other agents in the hallways. They all wear khaki pants and fleece vests meant to cover their holstered sidearms. It's a dead giveaway getup for federal agents trying to approximate the look of "regular citizens."

But I'd never seen her here. I'd remember if I had because currently there's a palpable "thud" in my chest, as she's asking me something else I only partially comprehend. Her crystalline-blue eyes are entrancing. They stare into mine with a sensual, unquivering intensity. I break her gaze briefly to take in those lips, which I'm already imagining kissing.

We talk for a several minutes as I willfully ignore Brian's earlier request that I hustle because he's starving.

Then I muster just enough composure to suggest that we meet later that afternoon at the bar in the same restaurant Brian and I are going to for lunch.

She agrees, flashing me a smile. I make a half turn hoping she doesn't see me check out her exquisite behind.

I head back to Brian's office.

"You know those Diplomatic Security folks down the hall?" I ask Brian.

"The ones in the vests?" he asks.

"Yeah. I just met a gorgeous one."

Amid the downtown, happy-hour revelers, we sit at the bar and talk about our jobs and common interests, both of which intersect at international affairs and a healthy distrust of world leaders. I stare helplessly into those eyes and listen to her explain the duties of a federal agent that she is permitted to tell me about. She talks vaguely of investigations, undercover work, training with automatic weapons, and some of the visiting world leaders she's guarded. Amid her tale of watching over the Israeli foreign minister, I realize I'm deeply smitten. As she talks about her previous life as a lawyer, a halo of my enchantment appears to envelop her. She could tell me she knows who killed Kennedy and I would smile and nod like a moron.

*I really want to touch this woman.*

Maybe just one of those forearm brushes that women employ to show they're interested and men in turn often interpret as "How far is your place from here?"

But I can't, even though I'm drawn to her as strongly as I've ever been drawn to a woman.

The reason I can't is because I have a girlfriend. We've been together, on and off, for a year. She's lovely. Kind and beautiful. But lately our relationship is showing undeniable signs of fatigue that likely indicates we're not meant for the long haul.

I blurt out something about my girlfriend because I'm sensing it's the question on both our minds.

"Oh, I have a boyfriend," she tells me in a simple retort that I then mentally parse syllable-by-syllable for clues to the seriousness of said relationship like it's the Zapruder film.

*Did she disclose her relationship status reluctantly or is that just wishful thinking on my part?*

I sensed a tone of regret in the last syllable of "boyfriend" as if theirs is a casual relationship devoid of staying power. Or maybe that's just hopeful interpretation.

We keep talking as if our mutual admissions were merely a matter of clearing the air of any potential romantic misunderstandings on either of our parts. But the subtext is undeniable.

*There's heat here. I'm definitely not imagining it.*

*Wait, am I?*

We walk out together and say our goodbyes on the sidewalk. I tell her how glad I was to meet her. She, likewise. Halfway between a handshake and a hug we settle into the latter, holding our embrace longer than close friends. Her chin is buried into the back of my neck.

*Definitely not imagining it.*

# CHAPTER 4
# A "HURT LOCKER" SITUATION
SEPTEMBER 8, 2010
KUNAR PROVINCE, EASTERN AFGHANISTAN

A local Afghan man says there's an IED in the road not far from PK. A platoon is going to check it out so I tag along to grab additional elements for my story. Finding an explosive device—before it blows, of course—is always sexy.

I also jump at the chance to go out because I'm desperately in need of a distraction. I've been sitting around all day stewing over why my fiancée hasn't written back to me. I've checked my email a half dozen times since last night. Nothing. I sent her a new message early this morning. I hope she's just pissed and nothing's wrong. And it's not like I can call her from out here—no coverage on my Afghan cell. The Taliban often control the rural cell towers, shutting off coverage at will. Their indifference to my relationship woes is irksome.

It's a bumpy ride to get to the IED along a dirt road flanked by a river running fast with muddy, foaming water.

When we near the site where the bomb is buried, the trucks stop short and everyone files out except the drivers, who keep the vehicles running in case we need to beat a hasty retreat. I'm careful not to step anywhere that looks freshly dug up, placing my feet in the exact same spots as the guy in front of me. No telling what's out here and where it's buried. Situations like these give me the heebie-jeebies. My greatest fear is getting blown up and surviving the blast without one or more of my legs. I've given this lots of thought—I'd rather die on the spot than live a long life in a wheelchair.

The guys don't seem all that worried as they approach the spot in the road where the Afghan man says the IED is buried. I try to affect the same casual attitude while secretly freaking out at the possibility that the whole area is laden with explosives waiting to take us out.

The platoon takes up positions along the road to secure the area against potential Taliban attacks and direct a handful of drivers trying to get through the IED zone.

"Bomb! Bomb in the road!" Zotto says to a group of onlookers who stepped out of the vehicle to better eyeball the situation. They stare at him blankly, as if they have no idea what he's saying. Zotto's sweeping arms gestures miming an explosion don't seem to be helping.

"It's probably these assholes that were freaking planning to blow us up," he says while smirking. "They saw we were down here and they wanted to come see what was up."

He tells me that the tipster who pointed them to this location said he also knows where the IEDs were planted by a nearby bomb-making cell comprised of several high-school-aged boys. "They get them while they're pretty young." I contemplate just what might be the right age to begin one's bomb-making apprenticeship and whether typically scatterbrained, hormone-raging teenage boys are the best candidates for constructing explosive devices.

The rest of the platoon is scouring the slope on the right-hand side of the road, searching for the command wires the tipster now says lead to three separate IEDs in the road spaced about a dozen yards apart. Some IEDs must be detonated by someone on the other end of a long wire when a vehicle passes over them. Touch the end of the wire to a battery that sends a charge down the length of it to the explosives buried in the road and presto—engine blocks and bodies go flying through the air.

Spc. Wyckoff finds a poorly concealed wire tucked under a few small rocks. "They get really fucking obvious with it sometimes," he says, pointing to a line of stones leading down to the road where the IEDs are buried.

I follow the wire back down to the road where, Zotto is shuffling some dirt around with the toe of his boot to expose the copper line. This doesn't strike me as something one should jiggle so casually. But I shoot some video of him prodding the wire anyway, hoping it's not the footage cable news shows on repeat to illustrate the dangers of IEDs when they deign to cover the war on weekends at 2 a.m.

This situation calls for an expert touch, so guys call in the EOD technicians to handle the removal of the bombs. EOD, or Explosive Ordnance Disposal, are the military bomb unit some folks back home are vaguely familiar with because of the *The Hurt Locker*, a movie about a plays-by-his-own-rules military explosive tech who always sports a thousand-yard stare and had a box of stuff under his bed that makes him sad or something. I forget all the details.

After the real-life EOD shows up at the scene one of their techs dons their trademark, full-body ballistic gear: a cross between a hunter-green astronaut suit and one of those puffed-up, fully-body sumo wrestler getups popular at corporate parties where drunk office drones get to wail on one another.

I film from a distance as he maneuvers his awkward mass to the site of the explosive and traces the first wire to a hole just alongside the road. After a few minutes of prodding, he discovers there are no explosives—just a bag of rocks. It's a dummy bomb.

*Whew!*

My relief is short-lived, however. There are still two more wires to examine. He traces the second one to another hiding spot along the road. At the end are more rocks wrapped in a dirty, white cloth. Another fake.

*This has got to be pissing him off. All dressed up with nothing to do.*

Before investigating the third one, the EOD takes a break and removes his bulky suit to catch his breath. He's covered in sweat due to the stifling bulk of his protective gear. I give him a few moments to relax, then approach, telling him I'm a reporter. Right off the bat he says he doesn't want to talk or be filmed. I tell him we can talk off the record. There's really just one thing I want to ask:

"What did you think of *The Hurt Locker*?"

This of course is a loaded question for anyone in EOD. The cinematic depiction of a rogue bomb defuser and just a few guys heading out all alone to dismantle enough explosives to level all of Baghdad pisses them off.

I get their annoyance. Sure, I love Kathryn Bigelow's over-the-top cinematic antics in *Point Break,* a movie whose clunky dialogue I can quote chapter and verse ("*Utah, get me two*"), but *The Hurt Locker* is just ridiculous.

The EOD's roadside movie review is an expletive-laden tirade about the film's cartoonish action sequences that has me in stitches.

As promised, I don't record or write down a word.

I do, however, tell the guys from PK pulling security along the road what I asked him. They know how touchy EOD are on the subject and start busting balls over the radio.

"We have a Hurt Locker–type situation here, over," quips one of the soldiers in a faux-serious tone while trying to suppress a giggle.

"Tell Hurt Locker to hurry it up so we can go home, over," says a voice on the other end.

The third and last wire doesn't lead to another bag of rocks. Instead, it's connected to a large orange watercooler filled with about a 100 pounds of explosives. It's HME, Homemade Explosives, in this case ammonium nitrate fertilizer used on crops. It's been banned in Afghanistan for this very reason. Loads of it are secretly trucked in across the border from Pakistan every day.

One hundred pounds probably wouldn't be enough to obliterate the armored vehicles the guys from PK ride in. But this amount could pierce the reinforced steel hull and send hot, jagged shards of metal flying into the vehicle, shredding flesh and bone. And if the blast hits just so, it might even tip a truck right into the river, potentially drowning everyone inside. That's unfortunately happened to US soldiers in the past.

EOD has a plan for getting rid of the bomb on the spot. They carefully disconnect the wires from the cooler and gently extract it from the ground. Then they carry it to the rocky river bank to do a "controlled det," or detonation.

They attach their own explosives, C4, to the cooler and instruct us to all move back.

I take a position about 50 yards away on a small ridge overlooking the road, hoping to get a good shot of the explosion with my video camera. They better do this soon—the sun is about to set, and without good light this explosion won't be nearly as sexy the visual as I'm expecting it to be.

Lying on my belly, camera aimed at the road, I'm getting anxious.

*Let's light this sucker already. Daddy needs a big boom.*

Someone shouts three warnings in quick succession:

"Fire in the hole!"

"Fire in the hole!"

"Fire in the hole."

A hair in time before I hear the blast, a cloud erupts from the cooler. Then a roar fills the air, making my ears ring and head feel momentarily concussed. A large boulder is ripped from the river bank and flung into the water.

A moment later, a fine trickle of debris, tiny rocks pulverized by the blast, rains down on me, plinking off my camera and my helmet, inside of which my head is still vibrating.

*That was pretty sexy.*

The first crack of gunfire catches me off guard and echoes through the river valley, whizzing above our heads.

"It was hitting across the fucking river, right over there!" someone yells to Zotto.

A couple more shots ring out in the twilight. I can't tell the direction. Then, silence, except for the steady thrumming of the armored trucks' engines.

Pop shots in the dark are unnerving, but not nearly as worrisome as what Zotto then tells me. "We just got word that we went over an IED on the way out here. So it might go off on our way back."

"It's going to be a long night," I say, feigning a cavalier attitude toward the prospect of riding back to PK in the dark with a deadly explosive lying in wait for the potentially unfortunate among us.

As the trucks slowly creep along the dirt road, each bump makes my stomach twist in anticipation of the blast that will send me into oblivion. I've nearly sweat through my body armor by the time we reach the gates of PK, back to relative safety.

I drop off my gear and go check my email.

Still no message from her.

# CHAPTER 5
# MEAN MUGGING
SEPTEMBER 9, 2010
KUNAR PROVINCE, EASTERN AFGHANISTAN

Marijuana can take root just about anywhere in Afghanistan where there's a fistful of dirt. It is a weed, after all. Cracks in walkways and rocky patches contain just enough soil for it to flourish. I've seen it sprout out of earthen walls on US bases and next to the barracks of Afghan soldiers who, when asked if they smoke dope, deny it with a rousing and well-rehearsed (tongue-firmly-in-cheek) chorus of: "Hashish . . . no good!"

There's a helluva lot of weed growing here in Gewi, a small village just a few miles down the road from PK. While walking through one clump of reefer, I make sure to capture it on film for my video piece. I want to include a few prolonged shots of the guys among the marijuana without making any reference to it—see if anybody notices. But the soldiers are laughing as we march single file through the doobie thicket.

"Are you looking at what you're walking through right now?" Wyckoff asks me snickering.

Meanwhile, shots ring in the distance, followed by the hollow boom of mortar rounds. There's fighting on the other side of the mountain. No one seems too concerned about the artillery except for me. Creeping terror makes my legs jangle again. I can't let the guys see I'm rattled, so I affect an air of nonchalance.

"The marijuana? Oh . . . Yeah," I reply. As if I wouldn't recognize weed—I probably smoked twice Wyckoff's body weight in dope by the time

I was his age, which based on his baby-faced features I'm guessing is somewhere around 19.

While I grab close-up shots of the aromatic buds, Zotto and Wyckoff peel off for a confab by the side of the road near a handful of stone and mud homes. There's another explosion in the distance, this one louder. "There go the rockets," says Zotto. I decide to stick near him out of some misguided logic that the platoon leader is less likely to get killed if the shit pops off.

The other soldiers return to the narrow dirt road running through Gewi, where Zotto and I approach a group of locals for a chat. Judging by the scowls on their weather-hardened faces and contemptuous glances, they aren't all that jazzed to see us, let along gab. There's probably a good reason for that. It's the last day of Ramadan and villagers are preparing for the multiday feast that marks the end of a month of fasting. This year Ramadan occurred during the hottest part of the summer, making abstention from food and especially water a torturous show of faith. Now that it's over, this day is supposed to be one of joyous relief and celebration after a long, arduous religious observance. With us walking through their village on such a holy day, I'm guessing feels to the locals like we're shitting all over it.

A few of the older men in the village are giving us a good "mean mugging," the dirty look some Afghans give soldiers when they wander into their midst uninvited—like we're doing right now. I try to lighten the mood with a group of younger men sitting on the side of the road. Video camera in hand, I ask them how they're doing, then clumsily segue into whether the Taliban has visited their village lately. It's a dumb question—these guys would never tell me if the Taliban were there. In fact, some of them probably are Taliban, or at the very least Taliban supporters.

A handful of Afghan boys scatter when I try to say hello. Youngsters are usually a pretty good indicator of the vibe in a village. If the kids are friendly, slapping high fives and shouting what few English phrases they know, there's a good chance some men might be receptive to talking. No chance of that here. Their fleeing just now is a bad sign. The older men meanwhile continue to keep their distance. Others retreat into their homes. I'm getting a really hinky vibe about this place.

*Something doesn't feel right.*

I keep talking with the young men, training my camera on them while trying to keep my head on a swivel. Shooting video forces you to concentrate on keeping the shot steady and the subject in frame, robbing you of your peripheral vision. Out here, that's not good. I try to keep my questions brief, looking up at the road when they answer. The interpreter translates their responses, something about IEDs.

"IEDs . . . what do you mean?" I ask.

I'm so jittery I don't comprehend what he means by "IED" despite having filmed yesterday's controlled detonation of a homemade explosive.

*Something is very wrong.*

In the camera's display I watch their eyes grow big.

*What is it?*

I look up and turn toward the direction of their gazes. Just down the road a dozen or so yards there is a man standing alone. He's facing us and carrying something on his shoulder.

*What the . . . ?*

A moment's confusion, followed by dread-induced clarity. He's shouldering a rocket launcher that's pointed right at us.

**WHOOSH!**

A rapidly approaching beeline of smoke races from his shoulder, followed by the rushing sound of blasting air. At the head of the smoke trail, a conical green rocket is screaming right for me. A few seconds of mayhem shatters into a million distinct moments of dread as I watch my approaching death.

The rocket seems to be trained just on me. Time slows down, confirming the cliché at life's final moments. I go from anguish over my demise to acceptance of my fate in a single breath.

*I can't move.*

*No point trying.*

*Just wait here.*

*It'll be over soon.*

**WHAM!**

The rocket hits me square in the face, a skull-rattling percussion that drops me to a knee. My camera falls from my hands and tumbles into the dirt road. My ears are ringing, my head hangs heavy against my chest.

*Did that . . . ?*

I tentatively reach toward my face with my right hand to assess the damage. I'm afraid to find out just how bad it is as I barely touch my throbbing cheek.

*Did that just . . . ?*

A gargantuan pain fills my spinning head as I try to comprehend what just happened.

*There's no way that just . . .*

The bells ringing in my ears would indicate that I am, however, somehow, still alive.

*Wait . . .*

*That's not right . . .*

*I can't be alive after getting shot in the head with a fucking rocket . . .*

*It's just not . . . possible . . .*

My attempt at rationalizing my continued existence is quickly displaced by an intensifying typhoon of hysteria massing in my brain. Deep panicked breaths while feeling a wetness trickle down my fingers and into the palm of my right hand. When I pull it away, the blood pours from my face in a steady, thin stream that splashes in the dirt at my knees, creating dusty globules. All I can do is stare at it in disbelief.

The outside world is silent. No one says anything for what feels like a decade. Finally someone chirps up.

"Are you OK?" The inquiry sounds like it's coming from the far corner of a cave. It echoes inside my head.

I strain to formulate a response as the first wave of pain crashes into the side of my head like I've been clocked with a steel girder at 200 miles per hour.

"No, I'm not!"

It's all I can manage to say. My brain's been wiped clean of everything in me that's ever preceded this moment. All that's left is pain and fear.

An excruciating ache in my face pulls me from the sureality of my impending death into the aftermath of my survival as I begin to mentally assess my condition. First, the obvious.

*What happened to the vision in my right eye?*

It's not blackness I see, like when one eye is shut tight. Rather, there's an unfamiliar absence of vision, as if my right eye had never been there. I come to an immediate conclusion.

*The rocket knocked out my eyeball!*

Contemplation of the expulsion of my eye from its socket is interrupted when arms grab me and pull me to the side of the road. I see others grab Zotto with what's left of my vision. He's lying against a wall next to me and asking about his arm. The rocket apparently skipped off my face and hit him in the elbow.

"Where were you hit, sir?" one of the soldiers asks me. I can't see who.

"In the face," I tell him.

A hand holding folded gauze is pressed against my cheek trying to stop the blood. Others in the platoon scramble to take up defensive positions. Some get down on one knee and train their weapons on the nearby cornfield. The Taliban love using crops for cover when staging an assault. They could be coming for us right now. The others point their weapons toward a nearby hillside, scanning the slope for would-be snipers. Normally an attack like this is followed by a barrage of gunfire. It's a popular Taliban tactic: wound a couple, then hit the rest while they tend to the injured.

Several minutes pass without a follow-up attack. No sign of our assailant or any of the locals either.

"Do I still have my eye? Be serious with me," I ask Sgt. Grant Thomson, who instructs me to hold a piece of gauze against my face while he prepares to bandage my head. Thomson assures me in an eerily soothing voice that I still have my eye. I don't believe him, so I ask him half a dozen more times, each trembling query conveying my growing terror while wave after wave of pain surges through the side of my face. Again, I try to muster the will to feel with my fingers if my eyeball is still there, but can't bring myself to dig beneath Thomson's swaddling of bloody bandages. With my good eye, I scan the dirt road for any signs of an unclaimed eyeball or a blood splatter that would indicate the direction in which my eye may have been ejected after the rocket smacked my head. No luck.

If it has been knocked out, I'm not going to find it. We need to get out of here. There could be more Taliban on the way. Thomson escorts me by the elbow to a nearby truck for evacuation, offering me a final, if slightly agitated, reassurance that my eye is still in place after I ask about it again.

"Do I still have my eyelid?"

"You're not going to lose it . . . I can see your baby blue," he says, hoping perhaps I'll finally shut up about it. His inadvertent compliment about the hue of my eyes caught me off guard and for a moment I'm flattered.

*Aww, aren't you sweet.*

But it doesn't last long. Sitting in the truck I can't catch my breath. My diaphragm spasms and I cough up mucus-laced blood into the helmet resting in my lap. I feel like I might vomit, or choke on what's obstructing my airway. Gasping, I keep the vehicle's door open hoping some fresh air will help pass whatever's blocking my throat. "Shut that!" someone yells out. "They still might be in the corn!" I don't care. The truck is stifling.

*I need to breathe!*

Someone shuts the door for me and the trucks starts to roll. We drive a short distance out of the village. I learn from one of the guys we're going to meet up with the rescue helicopter called in to take us out of here. The brief journey is excruciatingly painful. Every bump in the road feels like I'm being shot all over again. The shattered fragments of my face feel like they're grinding against each other as my head swells with blood.

"I think my face might be broken," I tell Zotto, then ask how he's doing. It's the first time we've had a chance to talk. He says he's OK, then inquires about me.

"I've been better."

"I saw the trail of smoke," he says.

"So did I," I tell him, my first chance to recall the attack.

"Did it explode or was it a dud?"

I don't know why it didn't explode. It should have incinerated both of us on the spot. There's no way we should even be having this conversation.

The truck stops. Arms grab me again, guide me by the elbows across the road as the sound of whirling blades grows louder. A helicopter arrives and hovers over a farmer's field soaked in standing pools of water that shimmer and splash in the rotor wash. It strikes me that we're creating a very Vietnam War–esque tableau. Soldier and civilian banged up. I've got my body armor undone, dangling off my torso and covered in blood, my head wrapped in gauze that's already soaked through. All we need is Creedence Clearwater Revival, maybe a little "Fortunate Son" playing in the background, to complete the image of a war gone wrong.

Zotto and I are helped into the aircraft. I slump on the deck of the helicopter, weak from losing so much blood, and lean against the rear of the passenger bay, sending soothing vibrations up my spine as we take off. The roar of the engine prevents us from talking about what happened. No matter. I'm in no mood to relive it just now.

The medics are looking at me quizzically, as if the rocket is stuck in my head. They shout questions that I can't quite make out.

"Shadda, fladda madda, dadda," one of them yells at me, looking into my good eye, then pats me around the shoulders and arms, checking me for bullet holes or fragment wounds. He does the same to Zotto.

While he does, I look out at the shrinking Afghan countryside. I admire its beauty.

*I wonder whether this will be the last time I see any of this.*

Jagged mountain peaks washed in dusky sunlight. A river valley dotted by mud-brick homes and lined with small tracts of corn.

*This really is a gorgeous country.*

I vaguely ponder a future filled with lost eyeballs and facial disfigurement. Being half-blind and disfigured would certainly be a bummer. I don't have nearly enough insurance to cover a decent prosthetic or surgery to reconstruct my eyelid. I'll be a monster who prompts adults to avert their gaze and children to stare before they ask in loud, uncouth tones: "Mommy, what's wrong with that guy's face?"

I look at my cameras covered in bloody mud and figure I'm out several thousand dollars' worth of gear that I cannot afford to replace.

*Should have insured this stuff years ago. Stupid.*

There goes a big portion of my livelihood. I haven't been able to get by on just writing for years.

I wonder how I'm going to break this to my family and fiancée. I'm really not looking forward to explaining to them what happened. I'm terrible at conveying bad news, especially when I know I'll be thoroughly admonished for putting myself in a position to let this happen. When I was a teenager, I broke my hand and hid it from my parents for three days because I didn't want them to get mad at me. I had been drunk and doing front flips at a party to impress a girl when I landed flush on my left hand and snapped the third metatarsal. I reluctantly caved into the pain and confessed to my injury after my hand swelled to the size of a catcher's mitt.

*Maybe I can buy myself a few weeks if I tell my editors to keep it quiet. Yeah, that'll work.*

As for my fiancée, there is no telling what she'll say.

*Who knows? I'm not even sure she cares about me anymore.*

I could be getting worked up over nothing. Maybe I'm fine.

*It's probably just a scratch.*

That delusion wears off as the helicopter ascends higher, parallel with the mountain peaks.

*I'm not all right. In fact, I'm pretty sure I'm thoroughly fucked.*

I wonder if this is the end of my reporting career.

*If not, what do I do? Get a real job?*

*No, thanks.*

*If that's my only option, just push me out of this helicopter right now.*

# CHAPTER 6
# EYE PATCH—PORNO FANTASY
SEPTEMBER 9, 2010
SOMEWHERE OVER AFGHANISTAN

Hot wash from the rotors pours through the open doors of the helicopter, scorching my throat. "Can I get some water?" I shout. But no one can hear me. The helo blades' deafening thrum drowns out my pleas. I can't swallow. It's getting harder to breathe.

On the bright side, the morphine lollipop they gave me is taking effect, dulling the pain in my face to a manageable agony and curtailing some of my hysteria. The downside of the medication is that it's nauseating. Every time the aircraft banks a turn I feel a torrent of vomit threatening to make an appearance, though it never does. Throwing up would actually feel good right now.

We've already made several stops . . . I think. One was at Forward Operating Base Bostick, just a short ways away from PK. They unloaded me with a stretcher, looked me over, then put me back on the bird. Not sure what's going on. I ask, but the answers don't register. We stopped again. To refuel, maybe? I stay on board this time. Up, down. Back and forth. I don't know what's going on.

Then, after what seems like an eternity in the air, the helicopter lands at Bagram Airfield.

*Last stop. Thank Christ.*

Medics wheel me into Bagram's hospital, where doctors and nurses are brought up to speed on what happened. They ask me questions I can't answer.

Amid the mind-dulling morphine and the shock of being shot in the face, they seem to be speaking in tongues. I only catch their gist when they ask my name, if I know where I am, and what day it is.

"Afghanistan," I respond weakly, somewhere between a question and a declaration of certainty. As for the day—no clue. But that's not unusual. I often lose track of the date when I'm on an embed.

*It's September something . . . the early part. Weather's still warm.*

After assessing my recall abilities—with no baseline from which to judge, perhaps they think I'm not all that bright to begin with—someone produces what appears either to be the world's largest pair of paper scissors or hedge clippers. I'm not sure I like what's going on here. I feel the cool, blunt side of the blade travel the length of my chest and abdomen, then my upper arms. Then, starting at the neck and along the sleeves, hands strip my T-shirt into easily removable ribbons with a few deft swipes.

"Not the pants," I protest, "they are the only good ones I have left."

The nurses look at my blood-soaked trousers and into my good eye incredulously, likely wondering how severe my head trauma must be if I'm worried about them shredding a pair of muddy threadbare khakis. No use anyway. In seconds I'm as naked as the day I was born. I take comfort in my stark nakedness, knowing I'm svelte after a month-long diet of cheap cigarettes and little else.

A dozen hands probe every inch of my body, I'm assuming looking for errant wounds and bullet holes. It's oddly pleasurable. A guy would have to pay decent money for this kind of action in Bangkok. Here I am getting the royal Thai massage treatment on the house, courtesy of the US military and taxpayers. Instead of a happy ending, however, the hands-on attention takes a dark turn when one of the nurses (please let it at least be a female) jams a finger, way, way, waaaaaaaaay up my ass.

"Whoa, what's that for?" I ask in a high-octave protest.

"We need to check for spinal injuries," a male voice replies.

My less-than-heroic reaction to what's happening doesn't end there. Someone else jabs my arm with an IV. Due to my damn near debilitating needle phobia, I squeal like a schoolgirl before the soothing narcotic rush of pain meds turns my muscles into warm maple syrup. The universe slows down to half speed as the drugs make it easier for me to understand what's happening. Now, there's a doctor, at least I think he's a doctor, talking to me about the operation I'm about to have. He says something about repairing the laceration in the side of my eyeball. Apparently the blunt force of the rocket crashing into the side of my head ruptured my eyeball and caused the jelly inside it that gives it its lovely round shape to leak out and pour into my skull.

He shines a light into my eye. The beam illuminates the blood pooled in my field of vision. All I can see is scarlet with a black halo. In the periphery, there is light, giving me hope they can fix me. The doctorly voice says they need to go in, scoop out the jelly that leaked into my head, then put it back in my eyeball. That all sounds fine in theory, I figure, while trying not to imagine my eyeball dangling out of its socket while they backhoe the goo out of my head and return it to the inside of my eye where it belongs.

I have questions—too many to ask, though not enough mental horsepower to articulate them.

*What about my face? How screwed am I on that front? Seeing is one thing, but come on, being disfigured for life may be a bridge too far. Am I bleeding inside my head? What happened to Zotto? I don't remember him getting off the helicopter during one of our many stops. Where did he go?*

I'm trying to spit out my queries, but the sensation of warm, chest-compressing quicksand drags me deeper toward unconsciousness.

A moment later, I'm surrounded by a blissful, anesthetic darkness.

A thin sliver of light, then dark again. Warm tingling in my legs and arms. Limbs too heavy to move.

*Why bother? I'm comfy.*

I sink deeper into the mattress. A few moments later, or hours perhaps, I rouse again. Something splendid is coursing through my veins like a soothing, homemade broth. I've lost all sense of time. My one eye creaks open. White. Lift my head an inch or so. Feel the burden of an added weight. It feels like a comfy winter's cap.

*So snuggly.*

*Wait.*

*That's not right.*

*There's a needle in my right arm.*

Normally my needle fear would have me squirming out of my skin. Not now. Just so relaxed.

Looking down, I see a bed. At the end of the bed there are feet.

*My feet. I have feet. Check.*

Scrolling up top, I feel a bandage.

*What's this all about?*

I reach over with my left hand to gently test the firmness of the wrapping. It's billowy. The top half of my skull and the entire right side of my face are covered. OK. My arm glides back across my body and rests at my side.

*Something happened. Something bad. Bad things are why people end up . . . Where am I, exactly? Someplace remarkably clean.*

I was in Afghanistan. That, I remember. But this place is too spiffy for Afghanistan, at least the Afghanistan I know. A woman walks in wearing her pajamas. No, not pajamas. She asks me how I'm doing.

I muster a faint "OK," then I ask her where I am, how my surgery went.

*Wait. I had surgery?*

I'm surprised by my own inquiry, considering I'm not quite sure where I am or what happened to me.

She clarifies: "Yes, there was a surgery."

*Got it, surgery. My surgery. I was hurt. Hurt in Afghanistan.*

I slowly start putting together answers to my own questions.

*There was a shooting, in a village, PK, Thomson helped me, Zotto was hurt, I was really hurt, and a helicopter came, then the screaming I couldn't understand.*

Like a laptop rebooting, my memories come online one at a time. I recall the last few weeks leading up to what happened. But while the nurse provides her prognosis of my injury, my mind starts to drift.

*Stay focused. She's talking about something important here, here in Bagram . . . I'm in Bagram . . . I was just here, wasn't I? That's right. I spent a few days here before Kunar at "Hotel California." I like the plywood shack where reporters are warehoused before embeds. Lounging in my bunk watching bootleg DVDs, working out and eating at the BBQ DFAC. I never get tired of ribs. Never, ever . . .*

" . . . lose that eye," the nurse says amid my remembrances of savory slabs of pork on the bone.

"Wait . . . what?"

"You'll probably lose that eye," she repeats matter-of-factly. The doctor, she explains, managed to retrieve enough of the eye jelly from inside my head (I have to figure out what that stuff is called), then put it back in my eyeball before sowing it shut. Despite his success, she says it's very likely the eye won't recover from the trauma. I think I understand what's she's saying, but I'm having a hard time rectifying how a surgery "went well" if I'm likely to lose my eye. I ask her name before she leaves, then immediately forget it after she says it.

*Well, this sucks. Just tell me I'm going to lose my eye, why don't you. Want to punch me in the dick while you're at it?*

This is upsetting news. But for some reason I can't conjure what would be the proper emotional response to losing an eye. I should be crying, clenched fists punching the mattress. Instead, I'm numb.

*It's got to be the drugs*, I rationalize through a persistent hallucinogenic haze that spawns another tangent of warm remembrance. This one is taking me far away from Afghanistan to fond recollections of my less-than-illustrious collegiate career. I spent much of the latter part of my university days numbing myself with the illegal variant of the opiate-based pharmaceuticals currently trickling through my body. It was the mid-90s, and Afghanistan was making its mark on the drug scene amid the ongoing civil war and the emergence of the Taliban. I, of course, was completely oblivious to the war in Afghanistan as I cruised the decrepit streets of North Philadelphia looking for the dealers least likely to rob a drug-hungry college kid trying to score junk. Now I'm here getting the sanitized, drug-company version of the stuff I used to buy on the streets. All the benefits of opiate use without the guilt and hassle of street-corner dealers trying to rip you off and beat you down. Now I know why so many people get hooked on pharmaceuticals. Bully for Pfizer for being so smart. I've got to buy their stock if I ever have any money.

*Irony, I guess.*

I fall sleep immersed in a fog of my past drug-related indiscretions thanks to the narcotics gently dripping into my veins.


When I wake up, I'm struck by the need to search for something positive to come out of this.

*OK. There's a bright side to this thing. What is it?*

First off: This little incident is just the kick in the ass I need to quit smoking cigarettes. It's been at least a day and a half since I had one, and I'm not craving nicotine one bit. So I've got that going for me, which is nice..

Now, as for my eye. I am probably going to lose it, just like the nurse said. I roll this notion over in my mind, and while I'm not thrilled about it, I'm not as upset as I imagine I should be at losing a pretty important part of my body. In fact, I've come to terms with my probable eye loss remarkably well. I've even come up with a solution already.

*I'll just rock an eye patch.*

Seems like a simple and elegant solution. As I ponder and eye patch existence, I begin to envision the actual benefits.

*Can you imagine how cool that will look? Ladies will love, love, love it.*

Alas, my fantasies of adoring hordes of women throwing their underwear at my feet and their taut, naked bodies into my eager arms prompts a stark reminder of the one woman whose adoration is not nearly as abundant as it used to be. I still haven't told her what happened. Or anyone.

*How is my fiancée going to react to this? Considering her opinion on my even being out here she might be mad. Real mad.*

*Stupid reality ruining my eye patch–porno fantasy . . .*

The nurse returns and gives me another dose of something through my IV that makes me feel even more cuddly and yummy, then a pill to kick that feeling into high gear. Basking in one of my best drug stupors of all time, she promptly kills my buzz by asking me whom she should contact about my injury. I consider telling her my fiancée, then decide against it, opting instead to tell her to just inform my editors. My parents can wait, too. No use riling them up while I'm in Afghanistan; I'll tell them when I get stateside. Eventually. Not any time soon.

When she leaves, I let my mind go slack so I can resume my enjoyment of the drugs gently escorting me back into blissful half consciousness.

*This is kind of nice.*

# CHAPTER 7
# HAPPY ANNIVERSARY, ASSHOLES
SEPTEMBER 11, 2010
BAGRAM AIRFIELD, AFGHANISTAN

"It's time to go," a voice says.

*Go where, exactly?*

I've been told once or twice already, I'm sure. But I can never remember where "where" is. I'm not even sure how long I've been here, at Bagram. Could be a day. Could be twelve, for all I know.

"You're going to Germany. Landstuhl," according to the nurse with the name I can never retain. Or maybe it's another nurse. There must be more than one. I don't know. These pain meds make everyone look the same with only slight variations. It's as if I'm being treated by a legion of scrubs-clad Cabbage Patch Dolls.

*What's Landstuhl?*

The word swirls in my head like a gooey caramel. *Laaaaawn-shtooool.* The nurse tells me it's a military hospital in Germany. Sounds good, I tell myself.

*I've never been to Germany.*

*Wait.*

*Yes, I have.*

*I was just there on a layover on the way into Afghanistan last month.*

*No. Two months ago. But it doesn't count if you don't leave the airport. I've been to the Charles de Gaulle Airport in France a dozen times, though never in*

*Paris. That's embarrassing. I guess I'm going to Germany. Why am I going to Germany again?*

I mean to ask the nurse, but I forget. That rocket apparent knocked every journalistic instinct out of me. Usually I can't go two seconds without asking "why."

She reminds me, again, that I'm heading to the American military hospital, where I'll receive follow-up care for my eye. Apparently the damage to my skull is also pretty bad. The rocket completely shattered the side of my orbital socket. She tells me that in x-rays it looks like dozens of fractured splinters because there are so many pieces floating around there.

*For now I'll forgo the grisly details, thank you very much, Ms. Kindly Nurse, whose name tag I can't read, even with my good eye, due to all the wonderful narcotics coursing around inside of me.*

*Just give me more of those happy pills.*


This gurney isn't nearly as comfortable as my bed, but since I'm apparently going for a ride I'll overlook its posturepedic shortcomings. It will be nice to see something other than that antiseptic, white room. As I'm wheeled out the hospital doors, I breathe deeply the complex bouquet of aromas Bagram has to offer: jet exhaust, burning trash, and just a hint of fecal matter. Still, it's good to be outside.

They load me onto a vehicle for a short ride to the flight line, then wheel me onto a waiting plane bound for Germany.

There are others on the plane. Like me. Each one on a gurney. They are soldiers though. Injured soldiers. Some soldiers with injuries much worse than mine. I can tell because of the way their handmade quilts lay across their bodies. Each of us has one. They are crafted by the caring hands of Midwestern housewives, replete with patriotic, apple-pie images from back home. My quilt covers my torso, tapers down to my legs, then pops at the tips of my toes. Two of the soldiers' quilts lay flat where legs should be.

I ask one of the flight nurses if I can keep mine; it'd make a cool souvenir, I tell her. She says no, then eyes me suspiciously, like I'm going to somehow smuggle this handsome handmade blanket off the plane in my rectum.

We take off. Someone gives me pills that thicken the dense head fog in which I now permanently exist. The plane vibrates rhythmically after leveling out, lulling me to sleep like an infant on a long car ride. When I wake up midflight, there's a soldier next to me asking, "What day is it?" to no one in particular. Barely audible above the whirl of the plane's propeller-driven engines, a voice says, "September 11." There is a collective groan in the plane.

*Thanks again, bin Laden. Yours is the gift that keeps on giving.*

I'm a curiosity here in Germany, it seems. Every doctor at Landstuhl is stopping by my room to hear the story about the reporter who was shot in the face with an RPG and didn't get killed. I, of course, dig the attention. Recounting what happened, and surveying the reactions of those I tell, I'm starting to comprehend just how fortunate I am to be alive. Had that RPG detonated, what would be left of me would fit neatly in a matchbox.

There's a plan for me here, it seems. The doctors (*Why can't I fucking remember anyone's name? As soon as I hear one, it's lost in the smog between my ears*) say I have to spend a few days here to see how my eye is reacting to the surgery. A tousled blonde doctor removes my bandages and a plastic eye shield to shine a penlight in it. I feel the heat of the beam and can make out faint traces of white light. He says it looks good. Good meaning it just might be salvageable, meaning maybe there won't be a gaping hole in my head where my "baby blue" used to be. This is surprising news, I tell him, considering the prognosis I received in Bagram.

"Diminished expectations," he says of their original assessment. Doctors start with the worst-case scenario so patients, in theory, can come to accept their loss or imminent demise, then upgrade their prognosis if they manage to improve. Makes sense, I guess, but it seems more like the kind of ass covering they're taught in medical school to ward off potential lawsuits. Feeling good about what I heard, I walk back to my room with a nurse escorting me by the elbow. I'm even relatively steady on my feet. Not so bad. I might even come out of this OK.

*Suck a dick, Taliban.*
*No. Wait . . .*
*Suck a whole bag of them.*

I have a visitor. He comes into my hospital room and greets me, bearing gifts. Bags of clothes. I know this guy. He certainly knows me. I light up with recognition when he greets me, but for a moment I'm drawing a blank. I feign recognition while my mind races to remember who the hell he is. It's a trick I perfected during my heavy booze days. People I met while drunk, then later ran into when I was relatively sober, would remain complete strangers several minutes into our conversation until they provided just enough contextual clues for me to scour the recesses of my previously plastered mind to piece together their identities. I call it "the drunkard's art of deduction." The trick is not letting the forgotten notice you're trying to figure out who the hell they are.

I'm using that trick now.

*That's right. Smile and nod. Laugh when he laughs. Buy yourself some time so you can figure it out.*

After just a few seconds, I have it. Bam! It's Ben Plesser, a producer for CBS. I know him from Miami. He worked there for a while. Now he's based in London. He flew to Germany to help me. And he's come bearing gifts.

Ben shows me bags of natty new threads, which is good because I have nothing to wear but a hospital gown that, stereotypically, doesn't cover the entirety of my ass. He also has news, which is even better because I have no idea what's in store regarding my uncertain future and the fate of my fractured face and ruptured eye.

He says CBS is flying me to New York for surgery at Columbia University Presbyterian Hospital in Manhattan, where a team of doctors is already trying to figure out the best way to save my eye and repair my face. Alongside Ben is a civilian nurse who tells me his name, which I instantly forget. He will escort me on my flight to New York, administer my pain medication along the way, and make sure I don't drop dead from some yet-undetected embolism sloshing around between my ears.

There's a plan. A course of action. I'm psyched by all this activity on my behalf.

Ben gives me his phone to make some calls—mine, and the rest of my stuff, is still back at PK. I can't put this off any longer, I tell myself through gritted teeth and residual Catholic guilt. I need to let people know what has happened to me. I really don't want to tell anyone about this right now, particularly my parents. I'm still that teenage boy afraid to admit he broke his hand, except now I'm 36 years old. Pathetic.

I muster the courage to call my fiancée.

"Hon, it's me."

"Who?"

"Uh, me . . . Carmen."

"Oh, I couldn't hear you."

I proceed to explain in the simplest terms possible that I'm not in Afghanistan, that the most unlikely thing imaginable happened to me, and though I'm pretty banged up and facing the loss of an eye, I'm as fortunate to be alive as any human being in the history of human beings.

"Have you told your parents? They called me because they hadn't heard from you in a while and thought I had. I mentioned we were having problems. Did you not tell them?"

That I hadn't shared with my folks the intricacies of my recently troubled love life is not my main concern at the moment. I am, however, concerned that she doesn't seem that worried about me. Instead, she admonishes me loudly for not informing them first.

"I'm not telling them what happened to you! You need to take responsibility!"

Not the reaction I was hoping for, though considering the friction in our relationship of late, I shouldn't be surprised. Those therapy sessions we went to a few months ago did not work one bit and cost me a thousand bucks. I'm still kicking myself for taking advice from a 25-year-old relationship counselor without nearly the amount of emotional scars necessary to understand the dumpster fire that our relationship had become. I tell her I'll let my parents know right away, then promptly renege on that promise.

*Only one ass whooping per day for me, thank you very much.*

# CHAPTER 8
# THIS IS MY SAFETY
SEPTEMBER 5, 2009
ROCA SUNZAL, EL SALVADOR

It's been months since our long embrace outside the Claude Pepper. I think about her a lot, replaying our encounter over and over, and wondering what might have been were the timing right. We had a connection, stronger than any I've had during the three years I've lived in Miami. More than my last girlfriend, and certainly more than the one before her.

I haven't seen my foxy federal agent since, not that I'm avoiding her. I'm just not spending as much time in Brian's office these days. The last few months I was in Haiti and India for work. But my trip to El Salvador is strictly for fun.

I love this place. A photographer friend and fellow surfer introduced me to the country years ago. It's got the best point break surf in Central America. We'd surf in the mornings, then in the afternoons drive to the slums of the capital to interview gang members for a story. They were covered in tattoos and sported hard stares, but most ended up being really cordial. Sure, some had more than a few murders under their belts, but they were gracious hosts, inviting us to their modest homes to talk.

Every time I return to El Salvador, I fantasize about setting up shop on a small piece of land near the water and living out the rest of my days as gringo surf bum. But seeing as I've got less than a grand in the bank and credit card debt coming out of my ears, midthirties retirement is just a pipe dream. A week's worth of surf is all I can afford for now.

When I'm through here I head back to Miami, tie up some loose ends, and pack my bags for Afghanistan to cover the US troop surge already underway. I squeezed this surf trip in before going because I like to treat myself before a potentially dicey assignment figuring I might not come back with all my parts, or at all. It's unlikely, but still. It's a good excuse to go surfing. Not that I need one.

Today's session was epic. I caught several long, carving waves before paddling in for a hearty breakfast of eggs and spicy black beans, followed by Salvadoran-style pancakes and a *café con leche*.

My belly full and my body fatigued from my morning session, I head back to my hotel room to relax and check my email while gently rocking in the hammock on my balcony.

*What's this?*

It's a message from her:

**xxxxxx@hotmail.com**
**I just wanted to say hi and see how you're doing. It's been a while.**
**How have you been?**
**I recently broke up with my boyfriend, so there's that.**
**Hope you are well . . .**

*BA-BOOM, BA-BOOM!*

My chest leaps like it did the first time I saw her.

*Be cool. Don't respond right away. When did she send this? Eleven minutes ago. Answer later this afternoon. Better yet, tomorrow.*

I managed to let four minutes pass before telling her I'm in El Salvador, but will be back in Miami next week.

"Let's link up when I'm back. Sound good?" I write, trying to affect a nonchalance to mask my schoolboy enthusiasm.

She writes back immediately and says she's looking forward to it.

I am too.

In Miami, I suggest we head to a sports bar down the street from my place. I usually only go there on Sundays to watch my Steelers play. There she tells me her gridiron loyalties lie with Florida college teams, which I am willing to overlook because she's wearing those wedge high heels that drive me crazy. So sexy.

Over beers for her and Cokes for me, she tells me more about her life as a federal agent. Her work includes a lot of travel and often intersects with world events. So we have that in common.

And like me she has an appreciation for the absurd, talking about the time a high-ranking American diplomat she was guarding crossed paths at an event with Black Eyed Peas front woman Fergie. After their introduction and small talk about their respective musical tastes, she recalls how the two fell into an awkward silence she was forced to witness with a straight face while protecting her charge's life.

"After all," she says. "What are Fergie and Condoleezza Rice really going to talk about?"

Afterward, we head back to my apartment. She puts down her bag and places her work-issue weapon, a Sig Sauer with hollow points, on my kitchen counter.

"Can I see it?" I ask.

She takes out the magazine, checks the chamber before handing it to me. I look it over, feeling its heft in my palm, then notice something is missing.

"Where's the safety?"

"This is my safety," she says, curling her index finger and reciting one of the more memorable lines from *Black Hawk Down*.

My heart almost bursts through my chest before I kiss her.

She spends the night, asking to wear one of my T-shirts to bed.

"I'll only molest you a little bit," I tell her laughing, hoping to ease any potential awkwardness.

That, of course, is a lie.

# CHAPTER 9
# WORSE THAN I THOUGHT
SEPTEMBER 14, 2010
LANDSTUHL, GERMANY

Putting aside my fiancée's apparent disdain and throaty admonishment for the moment, I need to do something I've been avoiding. Though it's been several days since I was shot, I still haven't seen for myself what's under this bandage on my head. Based on the looks I've gotten from doctors and nurses who've examined me, it can't be good. Most do a half-assed job of masking their revulsion. They've certainly seen those worse than I: triple, quadruple amputations; faces burned off; and other assorted injuries from armor-piercing ordnances and IEDs. Still, it wouldn't hurt them to work a little harder on their poker faces.

I head to a bathroom down the hall for some privacy to look in the mirror. My hair is matted and filthy, still caked with dirt from PK and my own blood. I am drawn and gaunt. I can't remember the last time I ate.

*Geez, you look rough.*

The guy in the mirror has a face slack and grey. I study the lines in my forehead.

*Did I always have those?*

I carefully pull back the bandage swaddling the right side of my head, then gently lift the plastic eye shield . . .

It's worse than I thought. Much worse. There is a jagged train of stitches stretching from the corner of my right eye to about the middle of my cheek.

And that's the good part. My eye itself is nothing short of a hot mess. The pupil is blown out like a supernova, the edges of its blackness obscuring all but a tiny portion of blue in my iris. The socket appears askew. It droops noticeably toward my cheek. I recoil when I see how out of line it is with my left eye.

*You're permanently disfigured. This is what you look like now.*

It's a frightening prospect. People will stare and whisper, "What's wrong with him?" Strangers will recoil. I can hear that little shitbag toddler I imagined earlier asking his mommy what's wrong with me.

*Fuck you, kid.*

So much for looking sexy with an eye patch. More like I should be squirreled away at the top of the bell tower of some French cathedral. All I need is a hunchback.


Ben bought me skinny jeans. I hate skinny jeans and everything they represent: millennial entitlement, attention deficit disorder, playing the banjo ironically. And I just might miss my flight to New York because it's fucking impossible to run in them. We're super late. Little bit of a snafu this morning. First we drive to the wrong airport, then scramble to figure out where the right one is. Now nurse whatever-the-hell-his-name-is and I are booking as fast as my bed rest–weakened, skinny jeans–clad legs can carry me to the gate. We're in danger of missing the plane that will transport me to New York, where a team of doctors is waiting to conduct a series of invasive and unprecedented surgeries that will hopefully save my eye and perhaps return my face to a relative state of normalcy. Or, at the very least, make me decidedly less grotesque.

We arrive at the gate just in time to board, settling down in our business-class seats. Sweat loosens the tape on my eye shield, causing it to slide. The stitches holding my broken face together are poking out. If this thing falls off during the flight, my fellow passengers are going to jump out of their skins and pop the emergency exits. Man nurse helps me adjust the shield, then pulls out a syringe of painkillers to inject in the IV hidden under my skintight, roll-neck, zip-up sweater.

Nearly a week's passed since I was shot . . . I think.

*Five days? Has it been five days? I don't know.*

I'm haggard and emaciated, and in this ridiculous getup, I look like a German house DJ with a coke habit after a long night of record spinning and unprotected sex in the club's bathroom.

*Seriously, Ben. Not to be an ingrate, but right now I want to punch you in the wiener for picking this outfit.*

After my latest dose of pain-killing narcotics take hold, my ire slowly subsides, melting into delicious contentment and waves of warm humor, easing me into another bout of sweet oblivion.

# CHAPTER 10
# BEDRIDDEN

SEPTEMBER 16, 2010
NEW YORK CITY

My editor at CBS Radio, Constance Lloyd, is at the airport waiting for me when I land.

"You don't look so bad," she says cheerfully, though her face betrays a motherly concern and strain from several days of logistical challenges required to get me into the United States without my passport, which I'm guessing is still back at PK along with all my other gear.

"You look cute in those jeans," she adds. I obviously don't share that sentiment and fantasize about the moment I can strip them off and massage the blood back into my thighs.

I gather Constance isn't here to merely welcome me back to the States. I know I'm going under the knife again. This time for two consecutive surgeries. I just don't know when. The first will, hopefully, further repair my eye. The other is supposed to iron the creases out of my crumpled head. CBS's medical correspondent, Jon LaPook, also a physician at Columbia Presbyterian in New York, is putting together a team of doctors at the hospital to figure out how to put back together the head of Humpty Dumpty, a role I played to great acclaim in the school play when I was six.

This seems all well and good on paper, but after a week of head-cracking injury and mind-altering delirium I'm wondering if perhaps this next set of surgeries can be put off. Maybe just for a week. I'd really just like to do something, anything that doesn't involve splitting my head open again like an overripe cantaloupe dropped on the floor of the produce section.

"Where we heading?" I ask before suggesting we play hooky and take in a midday matinee.

"It's straight to the hospital," says Constance.

*No such luck.*

Constance is imploring me to eat the food the nurse places in front of me. But as it smells like sacks of hot garbage peed on by alley cats, I decline. I tell her all the medication I'm taking makes me queasy, which is true. But I'm also fucking famished for anything other than this meatloaf, overcooked carrots, and a warm carton of grade-school-sized 2-percent milk.

She insists I eat something in a motherly tone that I know comes from a good place but is grating nonetheless.

"I saw a Wendy's across the street when we drove in," I tell her, hoping the fast food joint wasn't one of my many narcotics-induced imaginings. My first meal back in the states after a long Afghanistan assignment is usually a steak the size of my torso or a small pond's worth of sushi. But a bacon cheeseburger, salty fries, and a chocolate Frosty will do nicely.

She heads out to grab my food and I'm all alone for the first time since I woke up at Bagram, not sure where I was or what had happened. A little alone time is nice. This is what I was craving while being flown from one part of the world to the next and prodded by what seemed like hundreds of MDs and nurses.

*Lie back.*

*Take a breath.*

*Relax.*

But the bliss of a moment's peace doesn't last long. The first intruder is a flash memory of the rocket racing toward me. That smoke trail behind it, screaming toward my face.

*Wait, did it bounce off the ground, then hit me?*

I rewind my memory back to the shot, trying to recall exactly what happened. Then I get to the impact. The reverberations in my skull. The sickening sound. That moment replays on a continuous loop of torturous images I can't stop.

*WHAM!*

It clocks me again, blood pours between my fingers. I clench the sheets each time it hits. My palms are sweaty. My knuckles are white with tension.

*WHAM!*

The rocket connects with my face again and again and again until my mental angst is interrupted.

"Hey," says a lilting voice in the doorway. I look over and see a familiar figure standing there. Her I recognize right away. She's been one of my closest confidantes of late, though we've known one another only a short while.

"How did you know I was here?" I ask Tatiana as she comes to my bedside, a pursed smile on her lips, brown eyes framed by long lashes welling with tears.

"As soon as I heard I started calling around to find you."

*How'd she figure it out?*

I hadn't told anyone where I'd be. Very few people even know what happened to me. But I shouldn't be surprised. Tatiana is a good journalist. Crafty and resourceful. We worked together in Haiti after the earthquake earlier this year. She put together the team for *TIME* magazine's video coverage. She called me to shoot the devastation and relief efforts. We'd met only once before, when I stopped by the *TIME* offices in New York to meet with editors. We clicked right away, sharing the same passion for certain stories and ideas about what constitutes good journalism. We talked about the types of stories we might work on in the future. When I meet up with her in Port-au-Prince, amid the chaos of tent cities and dead bodies being pulled from the rubble, I remarked it was the first time I'd ever seen her standing.

"You didn't know I was this short? Is that what you're saying?" she said, catching me in an awkward moment and delighting in it.

We spent the next several weeks working together covering the horrors of post-quake Haiti and in a short time became close friends. One evening, after a long day of driving on earthquake-buckled roads partially blocked by rock-slides, she confided in me her concerns for the future. "I need to find a man before I lose my looks," she said with a smirk that couldn't conceal a semblance of seriousness in her quest for companionship. She told me she was envious of my recent engagement and I muttered something trite about her "finding the right guy when you're not looking." I thought she was adorable and interesting, but kept my opinions of her to myself, not wanting to breach some yet-unlearned protocol regarding the kind of compliments one can bestow on the fairer sex when you've just recently asked someone else to marry you.

At the end of our assignment, we shared a long car ride through the impoverished Haitian countryside over the border into the Dominican Republic. When we reached Santo Domingo, we checked into a luxury hotel. Sitting on a balcony overlooking the sea, just a couple hundred miles from Port-au-Prince, she broke down. Tatiana cried about the suffering she had seen and the guilt of being able to sit there in comfort and safety while millions were forced into tent cities, their homes reduced to rubble that buried loved ones. It was the first time she had witnessed anything that horrific. I told her to simply "let it go," as if she were fuming over getting a parking ticket, admittedly terrible advice for relinquishing the pain and guilt she was experiencing. But I couldn't wallow with her. Never allowing myself to spiral into depression about the miseries I've seen is a safety mechanism I created for myself that prevents me from falling so deep that I dive back into binge drinking and hard drugs. I just couldn't go there with her.

After Haiti, we talked almost every day while I was back in Miami planning my impending nuptials. Our friendship didn't go unnoticed by my fiancée, who balked at our frequent phone conversations and plans to return to Haiti together to follow up on the story that was largely forgotten by the news media as the months passed. Tatiana was the focal point of several arguments I had with my fiancée, though I assured her Tatiana was just a friend. And she is. But the assertions by my bothered betrothed make me wonder about Tatiana, occasionally, briefly, quite innocently. At first. Of course my imaginings eventually turned erotic, sending my residual Catholic guilt whirling into overdrive. I'd never do anything, of course. I love my fiancée and feel guilty about entertaining fleeting sexual thoughts that were not even my original conjuring. No, those were conjured up by my unjustifiably jealous fiancée, who, by the way, is not at my bedside. Tatiana is.

"How are you feeling?" she asks.

Tatiana hangs around while a succession of doctors and visitors drop by. All of them want me to recap what happened for them, including Columbia Presbyterian's chief of medicine, who also works with the Yankees. He gives me his card and I politely accept it, though am reviled by his willingness to be on the payroll of someone as contemptible as George Steinbrenner.

Neil and Danny B., friends going back to middle school, also visit. Both live in New York now.

*How did they find out?*

I'm about to ask them when Susan, who I've known since birth and just happens to be in the city on business, also makes an appearance.

News of my injury has apparently made the rounds back in Afghanistan too. Heidi Vogt, AP reporter in Kabul, reaches me by phone to ask me what happened.

"There were rumors that a reporter was killed. I just needed to check," she says matter-of-factly. "I'm probably not going to file on this."

I'm disappointed that my unusual injury doesn't even warrant a wire service brief.

A little while later, Shannon, a fellow journalist, and Dan McCabe, an outlaw cameraman, pay me a visit. Dan can't help but shoot video of my injury while the facial reconstruction physician, Dr. Eisig, comes in for his consult.

"Right in that little weathered slit," he says, narrating the action as a nurse slips drops into my eye. I know Dan well enough to realize his comments are dripping with sexual innuendo.

"That's a pretty sweet scar, dude . . . from the corner of your eye down to your earlobe."

"I'm gonna fuckin' rock an eye patch someday even if I don't need it," I say, giggling.

"El Carmen!" he says, crowning me with a new badass moniker. Dan is the ideal person to have at your bedside when you've been shot in the face. He thinks it's just the coolest thing in the world.

Dr. Eisig interrupts the banter of two man-boys to deliver some sobering news.

"Your cheekbone is badly fractured in multiple pieces and badly displaced."

Eisig goes on to explain that the incision in my face made by the doctors in Afghanistan isn't large enough to get to the affected area. So in order to fix it, he and Dr. Kazim, another member of the dream team, will attack the problem from another angle.

"We're going to make an incision in your hairline to get to the cheek-bone," he says, tracing his pen across the top of my scalp from ear to ear. He then says they'll repair the shattered area with titanium plates, perhaps also use bone shaved from the top of my skull, if needed. What he omitted—but it is apparent to everyone in the room—is that he and Kazim are going to pull my face away from my skull, repair the cheekbone, then sew my face back on. The gravity of the procedure doesn't hit me at first, but it must be serious. Even Dan is speechless.

Once it does sink in, and I'm sufficiently freaked out, I call my fiancée on a phone Constance gave me to replace the one I left at PK and ask her when she's coming. She says she can't get away from work, though she'll be in New York on her new assignment guarding Hillary Clinton when the UN General Assembly convenes later that week.

"Have you told your parents?" she repeats every time I implore her to come. This isn't good. I know it. I haven't, but she already knows that and has her weapon cocked and loaded. "I had to tell them. It's not my place. You need to take responsibility for this."

Normally, I'd have a snappy retort at the ready. But right now, I'm shooting blanks. I hang up and prepare to make the call I've been dreading.

*Here we go.*

As I'm about to dial, the phone rings. A 412 area code. That's Pittsburgh. It's my folks. I answer with clenched teeth and listen to my mother tell me through stifled tears what I already know—that my fiancée informed my folks of my injury. She scolds me for leaving it up to her to tell them. I listen for a while then end the conversation insisting I need my rest.

Tatiana takes this as her cue to leave. But I don't want her to go. I want her to take me with her.

*Stuff me in your purse and get me out of here.*

*Let's go back to Haiti where it's warm so I don't have deal with all this pain, relationship angst, and disappointment.*

She leans over to hug me, up on tippy toes so she can reach around my neck.

I relish her caring, nonjudgmental embrace, and feel her breasts against my chest. They're bigger than I imagined and quite firm.

*Deep breaths before the first strike. A knife flashes toward me. The blade slips neatly into my chest. I try to stop my faceless assailant from stabbing me again, but I'm too slow to react. The blade cuts into me again, deep ragged incisions lacerating my chest in rapid succession. After several blows, I stagger backward a few steps, then collapse. Hands clutching my chest, I breathe in, blow out. Blood shoots in long spurts from my wounds. I gasp.*

*One more breath . . .*

I wake up sweating. The room is dark. The door open halfway. Light from the hallway seeps in and the horrors of another nightmare are already beginning to fade into blurry memories. Distant murmurs at the nurses' station down the hall and the sound of rubber soles on linoleum. I turn on the TV for a distraction. Not much to watch in the middle of the night. *The Golden Girls* will have to do.

*Thank you for being a friend . . .*

*Travel down the road and back again . . .*

# CHAPTER 11
# LADY LUCK IS A SNEAKY BITCH

SEPTEMBER, 17, 2010
NEW YORK CITY

This place reminds me the orthodontist's office when I was a kid. Same taupe-colored walls, reclining chair, table covered with tools that look like torture instruments that stoke fear in the hearts of patients. All that's missing are the hobo clown paintings and barely audible Muzak crackling on cheap, built-in wall speakers.

Dr. Schiff is explaining the trickiest part of the eye-repair portion of the two procedures I'll undergo in a few days. He's the lead ophthalmologist and point man on seeing what can be done to save my eye. Schiff's short with silver hair that he wears in a teddy bear crew cut, the kind you get at the start of summer when you're eight. He's wildly enthusiastic in his presentation of what he'll do to repair my eye and obviously enthralled with the idea of working on such an unusual case. I'm guessing they don't teach "fixing an eye lacerated and decimated by an RPG" in medical school, so this is his opportunity to play a little jazz.

He says that in order to restore any of my vision he needs to go back into my eye, reattach the retina and inject a gas bubble that will hold it in place. After that, the body's natural healing process does the rest. However, for this to work, Schiff tells me the bubble must remain at the front of my eye at all times, right in front of the pupil. So to ensure it stays put, I'm going to have to keep my head straight down, pointed right at the floor, for four weeks. Eating, sleeping, sitting, peeing, whatever. Head down. To the floor. Four weeks.

"Sleeping will be the hardest part, but we'll make sure to get you something to make you more comfortable," he says, recommending massage cushions and conveying a buoyant optimism that he's hoping is infectious. I'm trying to catch it. But so far, I'm only guardedly optimistic and less than thrilled at the idea of keeping my head slung low for so long. Still, I reassure him I'll do whatever it takes to make his hard work pay off.

"So when you sleep face down, place your arms over your head like this," he says, stretching out on the floor of his office face down with his arms cradling his head, like a toddler who hides his eyes thinking it renders him invisible. He springs from the floor with the velocity of a much younger man and back on his feet with a comical hop. I can't help but fuck with him a little bit for my own amusement.

"Wait, can you show me that again?"

The Schiff-Eisig surgical show isn't scheduled for a few days. They say they can't operate until some of the swelling in my eyeball goes down. But they can't wait too long either because they don't want to risk damaging the orb by reopening old wounds that have already partially healed. It's a tight window of opportunity, which is something of a recurring theme for me. If I had just turned a fraction of a second earlier, the rocket would have missed me. A second later, it could have decapitated me. If the shooter had fired it from a few yards farther back, it may have had time to arm itself, removing me from this physical plane in a puff of smoke. Maybe if I had lingered a little longer in the bathroom of the Miami federal building I would have never run into my fiancée, who continues to be conspicuously absent. Lady luck is a sneaky bitch. You never know on what side the coin will land.

Until the surgery, there's really no need for me to stay in the hospital. Despite the severity of my injuries, I actually feel pretty good, mostly due to the bottle of narcotics jangling in my pocket and coursing through my bloodstream. Out of the hospital and left to my own devices, I have free rein to ingest as much OxyContin as I please, though I'm supposed to only take them every four hours. Or is it eight hours? Wrong both times. I check.

Twelve hours, according to the bottle. I need to be careful with these things. With my history of heroin abuse, I could easily slip down the rabbit hole. That fuzzy, laissez-faire feeling of mind-soothing softness that envelops you in warm sensuality and Billie Holiday melancholy is, well, super fucking addictive. Which is why heroin addicts will do anything to get their hands on more heroin. I would. Did.

I remember the first bump of dope I ever snorted with the fondness one feels for their first kiss. Heroin comes on quick, yet feels as tender and reassuring as a warm, familiar embrace. That is if you don't overdo it and get sick. Most people do. I didn't. I had a strong stomach for intoxicants built up over years of indulgence. The soothing waves of sultriness started in my head and crept seductively down my neck into my chest and extremities. I put down the rolled bill and slumped back, my more experienced friends watching me enjoy the greatest high I'd ever known. I remember feeling as if I were enveloped in pure love and seeing them eyeball me with envy. At the time, I didn't know why they were jealous. But by the next day I'd figured it out: the high would never be as good as it was your first time; that each time I partook, I'd want to do more in hopes of getting back to a place that no longer existed. After three days of using, I was already hooked and feeling lousy when we couldn't score on the fourth. Jittery and strung out, I was gleeful as the rest of them, some long-time users with full-blown addictions, when we were finally able to get more. I spent months riding heroin. Tried to quit once and got so violently ill that I contemplated going to the hospital. The summer I turned 21 I had no place to live and spent most of it crashing in a friend's basement, then in a tent in that same friend's yard when my presence in the basement was no longer welcome. Once booted from the backyard, I lived on the porch of a house where I once paid rent, but could no longer afford it because I was spending what little money I had on heroin. I went cold turkey later that year and spent two weeks in bone-aching, cold-sweat, dry-heaving agony. After that I tried to measure my usage, would go on the occasional, sometimes frequent, days-long bender, followed by withdrawal made tolerable by copious amounts of alcohol and weed. I kept that up for a couple of years, crawling to the finish of my college career and somehow managing to remain reasonably employed and outwardly functioning.

But that was a long time ago, before I moved to Cairo, running away from America to get the heroin monkey off my back and accidentally stumbling into a career in journalism . . .

Just lucky, I guess.

With a few days to kill before I go back under the knife, CBS puts me up in a midtown Manhattan hotel. I'm told to take it easy and limit my movement for fear that someone or something bangs into me and my eyeball falls out of my head or the shattered bones in my face fall even further out of whack.

I get squared away in my room, which doesn't take but a moment because the only things I have are the clothes on my back that Ben gave me and some pajama pants Constance brought to the hospital. It is the first time I'm not within earshot of a medic, doctor, or nurse since being injured less than a week earlier.

I go into the bathroom to take another look at my eye. It appears to be getting worse, not that I was expecting it to heal on its own. My right pupil is now completely blown out, giving me the creepy countenance of a soulless clown doll come to life to smother children in their sleep. The socket is still intact, though it seems to be migrating even farther south toward my jawline. The stitches have a fine crust of blood around each one. So much for sexy war wounds. Forget Quasimodo. I've gone full on Sloth from *The Goonies*. I try to muster a chuckle, but my voice rings flat.

Away from the hospital, I'm on my own schedule. However, I'm still pretty jet-lagged; my body clock is saying it's time to sleep when the sun's out. Not wanting to doze the day away and then be up all night with nothing but my existential angst to keep me company, I take a walk. It's a balmy late summer day in New York, one of the few times of year I can tolerate this city. Summers here are too hot. The garbage-juice stink disgusts me more than the open sewers lining the streets in Kabul. Winters in New York are no better. Lip-splitting winds swirling between skyscrapers that no amount of Blistex can soothe, black slush clinging to the bottom of car bumpers, suffocating puffy coats, gloves dropped in an icy puddle on your way to the subway—no thanks.

For all its faults, and there are many, I'll take Miami any day over New York, simply because there's no winter down there and their refuse is inexplicably less putrid.

New York is a rat's maze of concrete and iron. When I hear people here talk about their love for the city, I feel like I'm listening to addicts justify their drug of choice. This place is the most addictive drug of all, the cigarette of cities. There's no tangible high, just like tobacco, only addiction and craving that compartmentalizes your life into smoke breaks and subway rides. I'd rather be anywhere else other than this infernal island, but instead I'm stuck wandering around Manhattan, half-blind and hoping someone doesn't bump into my face, causing me to black out from the pain.

Midtown is in a tizzy over the upcoming UN General Assembly. Every other car seems to be a black sedan with a flag on it. Languages I don't recognize buzz all around me. And somewhere, amid this cacophony of ensuing diplomacy, is my fiancée. We spoke earlier today, this time on more civilized terms, and agreed to meet when she could get away from guarding Secretary Clinton in a couple of days. Her voice was softer, sympathetic even, the voice from when we fell in love. Nearly a whisper, somehow soothing and arousing.

Crossing the street a block from my hotel, I neglect to turn my head to the right, forgetting that I no longer have vision on that side. A black Lincoln Town Car comes to a screeching halt, its bumper inches from my knees, lurches forward on locked brakes, then sways back on its springs. The driver looks at me in astonishment at my stupidity. I mouth "my bad" and give him a half wave. In the windshield is the flag of Afghanistan.

*Trying to finish the job, are you?*

Karen and Lara come over to my hotel to cheer me up. Karen is a reporter for ABC News I met a year earlier in Jalalabad while waiting to go on our respective embeds. We became fast friends as is wont to happen in war zones, where there is little to do but gab with strangers during long, boring lulls in the action. After a few days of hanging out she asked me to pop a stubborn zit on her neck and I was happy to oblige.

Lara is Karen's coworker at ABC. One might consider her "quirky," if the word also implied a healthy dose of good-natured insanity. She wears aqua-blue–framed glasses and other oddities found in the closet of a rodeo clown but does it with conviction, so it works for her.

They rush into my room like gangbusters and plop down on my bed.

"We brought sexy nurses costumes, should we put them on?" Karen asks.

For reasons I can't explain and I know I'll regret the moment they leave, I decline. I'm not feeling it, which plants a seed of worry that my libido might be ill-affected by all the drugs pumped into me. I tell myself to just enjoy their company sans slutty nurse outfits and make a mental note to ask the doctors about the potential side effects of these meds. Even though I'd be in excruciating pain without them, some things aren't worth sacrificing.

Lara hands me a black eye patch she bought at Duane Reade, encouraging me to lean into my sightlessness. "I'm thinking this is going to be a good look for you," she says. Karen nods in agreement. We gab for a while about everything other than my predicament, then they take off.

Soon after they leave, Tatiana texts me saying she'll stop by after work. Her office is just a short walk from my hotel. I tell her we'll order room service and afterward she can enjoy one of my OxyContins with a glass of wine. Jokingly, I suggest we can watch some pay-per-view porn. Now I'm curious to test my junk against these pharmaceuticals, which have seemingly reduced my genitals to overcooked linguine. I can't remember the last time I was aroused.

"Sounds good," Tatiana writes back.


When Tatiana arrives we order liberally from room service.

"It's on CBS's dime so shoot the works," I tell her. "Don't cost nuthin.'" I'm constantly borrowing lines from movies to see if other's notice.

After dinner we lounge in bed and turn on the TV. Tatiana is enjoying her wine while the effects of the OxyContin I give her take hold. We slouch into the mattress, warm and snuggly like a couple of medicated bunnies.

"Are we going to watch a porno?" she asks, smiling hazily.

I'm pleasantly surprised that she brings up my suggestion and we select something that suits both our tastes. As the action heats up on screen, we nestle closer, my hand caressing her arms. She responds in kind. Our arms wrap around one another, then our mouths meet. We draw a long, slow kiss I can feel in my toes. Her lips are soft and giving. I pull her on top of me, running my hands over her body.

"I can't do much," I say, admitting my infirmities prevent me from making my efforts all that aerobic.

"It's OK," she whispers. "Just lie back."


I wake up the in the morning wracked with guilt and prepare a million excuses for what I did—none of them any good. Instead I resort to the kind of self-flagellation that comes so easily for those who attended Catholic grade school.

*You are a filthy dirtbag, you know that?*

So much for the OxyContin-hampers-your-libido theory. They should put a warning on the bottle: "May prevent you from responding to certain sexual stimuli such as slutty nurses uniforms, while not hampering others such as commingling with a friend while watching medium-core porn. Do not take while operating motor vehicles, heavy machinery, or are engaged, you cheating piece of shit."

Tatiana, meanwhile, seems fine. Bubbly, in fact. She giggles about not having planned to spend the night and says she wants to take a bath in my luxurious hotel tub. While she's soaking, I head to the lobby to pick up some clothes my friend Shannon left for me and contemplate my actions. I cheated on my fiancée. No getting around that. It is a shitty thing to do. I also just made murky the waters of my friendship with Tatiana, who I know from our conversations has had her heart broken too many times. This is bad.

But last night was amazing. Blow your hair back, give-me-seconds-please, incredible. Of course I should feel guilty. Then again, why should I? Extenuating circumstances, the likes of which are unique to my condition, allow me a transgression of this type.

Whenever I do something I know I shouldn't have, I start rationalizing like a lowdown, bus-bench lawyer.

I come upstairs with the new clothes while Tatiana is stepping back into hers. Her dark brown hair is tousled, bangs falling impishly over her forehead. She's wearing those cat-eye glasses a naughty secretary might wear in a porno.

*A porno like the one we watched . . . which led to us canoodling half the night . . . I'm the worst!*

The guilt is making me sweaty as Tatiana gets ready to leave. What exactly is the protocol for bidding adieu to a friend with whom you've hooked up? I've never figured that out. A high five seems off the mark. A kiss would be too personal and misleading. I'd like to kiss her again. She certainly looks kissable. I walk her to the lobby. Sensing my uncertainty, she reaches up, again on tippy toes, to wrap her arms around me and give me a long hug.

"I'll see you soon," she says, wishing me luck with my operation in a couple of days and promises to visit afterward.



In just a few hours, my fiancée is coming to see me. I check the bed for errant hairs and other signs of betrayal. Tatiana keeps her dark hair in a cute bob. My fiancée's hair is light brown and long. I straighten the sheets and take out the food trays. Then I shower, which is a particularly difficult task because I can't get my eye wet and certainly can't cover my head in a plastic bag like I might with a broken arm. More than a week since I was shot and I still have Afghan mud and my blood clumped in my hair.

After cleaning up, I don the fresh clothes Shannon left for me and lie on the bed. My jetlag, coupled with my lack of prolong sleep the night before, has left me exhausted. I can't let myself fall asleep now. My fiancée is coming.

*I'll just close my eyes for a second . . .*

A light knock wakes me on the second rap. I heard the first one in my dreams. I get up and answer the door. There she is. It's her. We've been apart for more than a month. Her eyes are blue like mine. They are steely and relentless when she's mad, tender when expressing love. Now they're cloudy. I can't read them, though can tell by her posture she doesn't really want to be here. She hugs and kisses me nonetheless. Her embrace is listless and devoid of passion. Her arms drape over my shoulders. Our torsos barely touch. She lets go almost immediately without looking me in my one good eye. She appears reticent to even enter the room.

Just a few months ago, before our troubles started, we would have thrown ourselves at one another with the reckless abandon of teenagers, intertwining amid tangled sheets. But now, there is confusion about how to act.

"How are you feeling?" she asks as almost an afterthought. I show her my eye and she grimaces, trying not to reveal her revulsion. "It's not that bad."

We then lie down on the bed, face-to-face, talking, not about us, but about her new duties protecting Hillary Clinton and being here for the United Nations General Assembly. When there's a lull in the conversation, we kiss. But each kiss feels hollow, untrue. I know she's only here out of a sense of obligation. I search her face for an indication she still cares for me. I can't find any.

I'm exhausted. The time change, drugs, my body's immune system working overtime to repair my numerous injuries. I'm wiped out. I tell her I need to rest. She snuggles up to me, her head in the nape of my neck. One arm behind her neck, the other wrapped around her waist, my hand slips into the top of the seat of her pants. For the few minutes, before I give in to sleep, it feels like old times. I drift into a light slumber, reminiscing about how we fell in love.

When I wake up a few hours later, she's getting ready to leave.

"Where are you going?"

"I have to get back to work. I'm on duty tonight." She has turned cold and says it's my fault for sleeping the whole time she was there. I walk her to the door of my room, then kiss her goodbye. She doesn't turn around as she walks down the hall and I close the door behind her.


"We need to talk," I tell her by text message.

"Can't. Busy," she replies.

"It's important," I write.

"Busy."

"It's about us."

"I can't do this right now."

I am compelled to push her because I don't want to lose my nerve. We both know it's over. One of us just needs to say it.

"Please."

"No! I can't do this right now!"

I write back. "I can't do this anymore."

"Fine, neither can I. I've had it with you! I don't know what I was thinking saying yes to marrying you. You're a joke!"

"Yeah, well your parents' house smells like a kennel," a particularly mean-spirited jab at her family in Florida with whom she is very close, and her hygienically challenged dog, Oreo.

This isn't my proudest moment, but I lay into her some more. She abandoned me when I needed her. She abandoned this relationship, turned on me because I'm a huge disappointment to her, a revelation of hers that predates my injury and forms the basis of many of her criticisms of me when we fight.

"You are not special," I begin. "You were merely regionally exceptional," a thinly veiled jab at her beloved home state and the dearth of sentient beings worth dating there.

"Fuck you! Don't bother me anymore!"

I don't reply.

*What else is there to say?*

I just broke off my engagement via text message.

# CHAPTER 12
# ARE WE CRAZY?
SEPTEMBER 19, 2009
MIAMI BEACH, FLORIDA

"I'm really going to miss you," she says, her arms and legs wrapped around me, face buried in my neck.

I kiss the top of her head while reciprocating her embrace. "Me too. Now that I found you I don't want to go." In a few days I'm leaving for Afghanistan. I plan to be there for a couple of months, maybe longer.

She and I have spent nearly every night together since our first date. We are as inseparable as two snakes intertwined head to tail.

*Isn't that how snakes mate? Seems right.*

I've had two girlfriends since I moved to Miami; neither of them really got me. The last one was smart, sexy, resourceful, but something was missing. I could never put my finger on it. I just never gave in to her.

But with my federal agent fatale, I feel understood and appreciated, even if we couldn't be more different and seldom agree on the state of the world. The first time she perused my bookshelves, she noted derisively the overriding theme of a collection of tomes about American intelligence failures and Bush officials' post-9/11 zeal for attacking Iraq.

"I want to check out your liberal propaganda."

Yes, we are on opposite sides of many issues; we debate constantly the efficacy of the Iraq surge and tenets of the Bush Doctrine. But that doesn't matter. I love our verbal sparring and am enthralled to be with someone who understands that there is a world beyond the clubs of South Beach, someone who yearns to travel and have adventures. I share with her my dreams, how I want to report big stories on a sweeping scale, the troubles I've faced trying to make that happen, my inconsistent and seemingly always-shrinking income flow. She gets it. She seems to get me.

The thought of leaving her is excruciating. I breathe in the crown of her head, then roll on top of her.

"Why couldn't I find you sooner? I've been in Miami for four years."

"I know. But when you come back we can be together all the time," she says.

Though I hate wishing away time, part of me hopes the next couple of months in Afghanistan go by quickly so we can pick up where we left off. I playfully grab her arm pulling her closer and she reflexively stiffens and places a hand firmly on my chest to counter the move. The hand-to-hand combat training she received while training to become a federal agent makes her a formidable opponent when we wrestle on my bed. On the rare occasion I can pin her, she claims she's holding back, has a quiver of secret moves that can drop me like a ton of bricks.

"Remember, your genitals are on the outside," she says wickedly.

After a few rounds on my mattress, we turn our attention to the disarray surrounding us in my apartment. Everything I own is packed in boxes. Not long before embarking on our romance, I actually decided to leave Miami. I'd had enough of this plastic town and its hollow inhabitants. In Afghanistan, I'd planned to figure out my next move, maybe stay through the winter until the next fighting season. But if I made enough money, perhaps I'd come back and winter in El Salvador. Or else someplace else. Maybe Southeast Asia. Somewhere warm and cheap with waves. My options were my own.

But not anymore. I'm coming back to Miami. Coming back to her.

I'll need to find someplace else to live when I get back from Afghanistan since I gave up my beachfront apartment already. In the meantime, one of her brothers is going to come over while I'm away and give her a hand moving all my stuff over to her parents' house. They must think she's crazy. I've only met them once and now I'm dumping my worldly possessions in their garage.

Had we gotten together a month sooner, I would have kept this place. But that's OK.

I don't care if I have to live in a refrigerator box on the street as long as we're together.

# CHAPTER 13
# HEAD CRACKED OPEN,
# CHEST KICKED IN

SEPTEMBER 19, 2010
NEW YORK CITY

On doctor's orders, I can't eat or drink anything for several hours before my operation. I don't care—I'm not hungry. I lie in bed watching mindless TV, unable to sleep. My nerves are frayed, thinking about what's going to happen under the knife tomorrow. I'm having two operations back to back, both of which require a team of physicians attempting some cutting-edge techniques. I'm worried about not waking up. I should be fine, but there's always a chance something could go wrong. A blood vessel could burst, rendering me brain dead. I'll end up languishing as a vegetable for years because some Jesus-freak group is lobbying for me to stay alive until their Lord takes my soul. Worse yet, I imagine being fully conscious while trapped in my body like the soldier in *Johnny Got His Gun*, unable to communicate and condemned to torturous loneliness with only my thoughts till I die.

Let's say I do wake up, and the surgeries went well, then what? What happens the next day and the next? A future that once seemed so certain is gone. "My fiancée" is now "my ex."

Then I get her message. It's a long email that I read, then immediately delete. But the damage is done. Phrases like "I've been seeing someone else much better than you" and "have fallen in love for real" feel like actual fist blows to my midsection. She writes that she's been cheating on me for months with one of her colleagues in Diplomatic Security and that I will be alone forever because no one cares about me. I can hear her mocking voice while reading her email, telling me I'm a loser who will never find someone, while she did so with such ease because "she's a good person" and I'm "a useless piece of shit." I take another OxyContin to dull my pain. I know I shouldn't. Her professions of love for someone else linger and reverberate like pure, pulsating agony.

I try to sleep, but I can't.

In the predawn darkness I catch a taxi to the hospital, check in, put on a breezy, back-exposing gown and prepare for the consecutive surgeries that my doctors say will take ten hours or more. Sedated in the pre-op room, my chest is heavy. My heart feels like it's struggling to beat. A nurse tells me to count backward from twenty. I barely make it to fifteen before crying myself into unconsciousness.

# CHAPTER 14
# A GEYSER OF GOLD

SEPTEMBER 20, 2010
NEW YORK CITY

*I'm thinking of a word.*

    *What's that word I'm thinking of?*

    *It describes how you feel when you can't possibly feel any fucking worse.*

    *It's on the tip of my tongue . . .*

The word is stuck in the recesses of my fuzzy mind, a nightmarescape of near consciousness. Just when I'm about to snatch it from the ether so I can describe my agony since awakening, a new wave of pain crashes into my already crucifying discomfort, creating a tidal wave of torment. For this feeling, I'm certain there is no word. There's no word in any language for just how bad my head hurts while lying here in the recovery room flat on my stomach, a fresh bandage on my pulsating face, neck twisted so that all the handiwork done to me over the last twelve hours can begin to heal.

    *I know I'm being a bit of a drama queen here, but this hurts like a motherfucker.*

    I also have a strange sensation in my abdomen and an assortment of tubes and wires spilling out of me like a preawakened Neo still slumbering in *The Matrix*. Not pain necessarily, but some kind of pressure. I'm reaching toward my belly with the hand not tethered to an IV to investigate what's happening down there when Dr. Schiff walks in. He says the operation went well, "very well," in fact.

After he completed his work on my eye, Drs. Eisig and Kazim were able to perform their duties, fixing the damage done to my face. Good news there, too. They ended up not filleting my facial skin away from my skull. Nor did they shear any bone from my scalp. With deft hands and tiny instruments, they were able to reassemble all the shattered little pieces of my cheek and orbital socket via my existing scar, which with a little luck will never be opened again. Once everything was put in its right place, they fastened the shards together with titanium plates, four in all, and a dozen screws. I'm excited by the fact that I don't have a shaved head or sheared skull and that my hairline remains intact. The idea of one day balding to reveal a zipperhead scar across my scalp was not going to make landing the ladies any easier, taking into account my other disfigurements.

Overall, I'd say I'm buoyed by this news. So are my parents. Through the gauzy shrouds of anesthetic and swelling pain, I see them through an open door, talking to a doctor and occasionally looking in on me. My dad comes in the room.

"Hey, buddy, how's it going?"

"Mmmmph . . . OK." They arrived in New York earlier that day. I'd asked them not to come until after the operation, which I'm certain upset them. But with everything going on with my fiancée—wait, ex-fiancée—I wasn't ready to deal with their reaction to the sight of me. I knew how difficult that was going to be on them. No one wants to see their child a mangled mess.

My dad then returns to my mother, who is speaking to someone I don't recognize and is crying.

Modern medicine is amazing. Following two major surgeries such as mine, I can go home after half a day's rest. It's either that, or the hospital just doesn't want me taking up a bed a second longer than necessary. That way they can do more procedures and make more money.

Hospitals these days seem a lot like restaurants, I surmise amid my growing curiosity about what's happening beneath my belly button. Just as eateries have to turn over tables to make more money, hospitals need to get asses out of beds as quick as they can.

I'm in the middle of working out the intricacies of my restaurant-to-hospital comparison and indictment of modern medicine, of which I am a very recent and fortunate recipient, when I'm told that I will very shortly be heading home.

*Home . . . where is that exactly?*

I checked out of my hotel room, so I won't be going back there.

*Home, Home, Home . . . ooooooh shit. Please don't tell me I'm being shipped to Pittsburgh with my folks!*

I'm not up for travel and there's no way I'm convalescing amid the inevitable onslaught of questions about my ex and the demise of our engagement while recovering on my parents' futon in the TV room of their apartment. Before I can inquire about future movement, a nurse appears at my side.

"It's time to remove your catheter," she says.

"Wait, my what?" So that's the pressure I've been feeling in my abdomen. Yikes.

"I'm going to need you to take a deep breath in, then blow out hard," she instructs me.

"Wait, wait, wait," I beg her. She's seemingly unmoved by my obvious reservations about having a hose yanked out of my penis.

"On three, breathe in, then blow out hard."

"One . . ."

*Holy fuck this is going to suck.*

"Two . . ."

*Really, really, really going to suck.*

"Three."

I breathe in with all my might and blow out with the force of Aeolus himself, hoping the power of my blast will mask the pain I'm certain the catheter's removal is going to cause me.

But it doesn't. Not. In. The. Least. The plastic tubing grates against the lining of my urethra as if I'm pissing rusty thumbtacks. Amid its agonizingly slow withdrawal, I emit a torrent of obscenities that would offend Larry Flynt. When it finally pops out my pee hole, a stream of my urine hoses the nurse down.

"Sorry," I offer weakly.

I'm not sorry. At all.

"Home," it turns out, is right around the corner from the hospital at 168th Street and Broadway in Manhattan's Washington Heights neighborhood. CBS rented an apartment for me there so I can be close to my doctors. I'll need regular checkups and follow-up care for the next two months. My dad tells me while a nurse helps me sit up that there's a car waiting outside to take me a few short blocks to the apartment. "Give me a second." Sitting up has made me woozy. I attempt to survey my surroundings, but Dr. Schiff reminds me not to lift my head.

*Oh yeah. That.*

Four straight weeks of staring at the floor starts right now.

*This should be fun.*

There is a bustle around me. I hear my parents and a host of other voices I don't recognize. I raise myself off the gurney. My legs feel weak, but they hold my weight. I marvel at my ability to stand, considering my head was just carved open and reconfigured like a jack-o-lantern one might consider too realistic and grotesque for the front porch.

"Easy . . . There you go," someone says.

I dress carefully, taking pains not to let the neck hole of my T-shirt even lightly brush my newly rebuilt and swollen face. Arms lower me into a wheelchair that rolls me down the hall. I watch the floor tiles scroll by. This is my perspective on the world for the next month. Outside the front door of the hospital, a car is waiting to drive me to my new home.

When we arrive at the building, there are people standing at the bottom of the stoop leading to the front door. I can see their shoes—sneakers and tan suede boots. I can only imagine their faces as they watch a partially wrapped mummy being guided by both elbows up the stairs to the front door. Someone keys in and I'm hit with the pungent aroma of a litter box in desperate need of changing. I shuffle along a hallway tiled with tiny ceramic octagons to the building's stairs. The marble risers are worn slightly concave from decades of climbing. We hike up three floors, each separated by landings cluttered with bags of garbage till we reach the door of my new abode. Someone keys us in. From what little I gather from my new waist-down view of the world, the apartment has a long hallway with a bathroom and bedroom on the right. At the end is the kitchen and spacious living room, off of which are two more bedrooms. It's way more space than I need and doesn't seem all that bad considering the refuse and odors in the stairwell. For a second I thought I was going to do my convalescing in abject squalor. Not that I'm a stickler for cleanliness. I've lived in some real shitholes in my time, though not while trying to recover from reconstructive facial surgery and an operation that hopefully, fingers crossed, saved my eye.

*This place will do just fine.*

# CHAPTER 15
# PROSTRATE IN NYC
SEPTEMBER 27, 2010
WASHINGTON HEIGHTS, NEW YORK CITY

"Mum, do you need anything before I go?"

"No, Franca, we're OK for now. Thank you for everything," says my mother, who hasn't stopped crying since her arrival in New York. I want to tell her to knock it off, but obviously I can't. I keep my frustrations on that front to myself.

*I understand you're upset, but come on.*

All my mother's bellowing isn't exactly bolstering my spirits. It's really bumming me out, in fact.

"Cry on your own time," I want to tell her. "We've got enough misery to go around here."

"It's OK. I'll see you tomorrow," Franca tells her, walking toward the door. With my head down I wave in the direction of her voice and offer her a half-hearted "see ya."

In addition to being my mother's emotional support system, Franca is a home health care provider tasked with looking after me while I recover. She calls my mother "mum" and my father "dad" instead of Laurene and Carmen (yes, I am a junior.) She lives in the far reaches of the Bronx and for a very short while after I was placed in this apartment she would spent the night here with me. But after a few days of sleepovers I grew tired of having someone hang around the apartment at night, though there's ample room. Her presence, while essential during the day when I need someone to run errands, comfort my mother, and keep the place in order, is unnecessary at night and grates on my already frayed and sleep-deprived nerves. Just knowing that she was in the other room, lying there quietly on her sagging twin bed while I fidgeted in my queen, irritated the shit out of me. So after a few days I told Franca she didn't need to stay, condemning her to twice-daily treks so long she might as well commute back and forth from her native Nigeria.

I spent quite a bit of time in her country covering the unrest in the oil-rich Niger Delta, where masked militants wielding machine guns and swilling bottles of brown liquor were hijacking oil shipments and taking rig workers hostage. I even had a couple of close calls in Port Harcourt, the de facto capital of the oil-producing region. Once, while walking along a narrow street flanked by a tall, expansive wall, a car steered right toward me, pinning me into a corner between the wall and the hood of the vehicle. The driver leaned over and said, "We're going to kidnap you."

Having never contemplated how I'd react to a kidnapping, much less one announced so formally, I didn't know what to do. So I just stood there, looking at my would-be captors with the blank, stupid stare of a witless victim ready to be scooped up and tossed in the trunk. The driver and his car mates glared back at me, silently assessing whether this American idiot they were eyeballing was worth feeding for the next few months while they sought ransom for my release. After conducting an on-the-fly cost/benefit analysis, the men apparently determined my street value far too low to justify the hassle of holding me hostage. So, they just drove off. That was pretty nice of them, actually. They could have just shot me in the head to make sure I didn't snitch.

I tell Franca this story. She's astonished that I wasn't hurt. "Oh, they could have killed you! You are very lucky!" she says confirming my previous assessment.

Franca's right. Come to think if it, why didn't they consider me worthy of kidnapping? Westerners were getting picked up all the time there. A few had been killed. But not me, lucky duck that I am.

I contemplate this good fortune later that evening while gingerly crawling into bed. Maybe tonight I'll finally get some sleep. It's been five days since my surgery and I haven't slept more than fifteen minutes. Lying facedown in my donut-shaped pillow, forced to inhale my recycled breath, I think about the nature of "luck" and whether I am the beneficiary of more than others, even beyond not being born someplace wretched and wracked by war, pestilence, and poverty like Franca's native Nigeria.

Discounting my being shot in the head with a rocket, I have gotten away with an inordinate amount of crazy shit during my life. Even when I was very young. At six years old, I would jump from the rooftop of my grandfather's dry cleaners onto the roof of the bar next door and onto the next building, and the next.

*Is that enough to prove my invincibility? Wait, am I onto something?*

Sleep won't come to me, so I keep staring into the darkness of my donut and contemplate the growing evidence of my seeming immunity to fatal consequences.

"This theory has some legs," I mumble, then recount later escapades as evidence of my infallibility. For example: One late night in college, while riding my bike in downtown Philadelphia, I was so drunk that I failed to notice a bus coming up on my right. Unable to maintain my balance, I weaved in front of twenty tons of steel and was hurled over the handlebars and into the street. Except for the skin of my palms being torn off, I wasn't hurt. The bus came to a screeching halt and the driver jumped out to check me, certain he'd just manslaughtered a cyclist. I offered him a wobbly wave letting him know I was OK, then hopped on my bike and pedaled home.

*That proves it. I'm infallible.*

I lie there basking in the deific glow of my newly discovered powers until I have to pee. I slowly rise from my bed and head down the hall. In the bathroom, I lift my head and treat myself to a rare glance in the mirror. Staring back at me is a decidedly less-than-radiant visage of stitches binding together the edges of a once-gaping wound and a dead eye.

I make a mental note to ask my doctors if delusions of grandeur are a side effect of the meds I'm taking and consider asking Franca to resume sleeping here—maybe just a few nights a week, in case my drug-induced perceptions of immortality prompt me to head up to the roof of the building to see if I can fly.

There's really only so much I can do in my present condition. Other than doctor visits, and the occasional foray outdoors when someone "takes me for a walk" around the block as if I were an infirm cocker spaniel with a cone around his neck, I remain in the apartment. I'm not supposed to exert myself. But all this hanging around doing nothing is causing my body to atrophy at an alarming rate. I feel as vibrant as a bowl of room-temperature tapioca.

The good news is that following my first postoperation checkups, my doctors told me that my eye is healing nicely and the bones in my face, held together with pins and plates, aren't shifting. I try to take solace in their assessment when considering how I've quickly turned into a perpetually stooped, pajamas-wearing shut-in—the homeless man's Howard Hughes.

In addition to making my midsection mushy, this sedentary lifestyle is also turning me into a real cranky prick. I'm fully aware of my short fuse, particularly with my parents, who are still in town and show no signs of leaving. They come every morning to the apartment and hang around till early evening, then head to my Uncle Billy's house on Long Island, where they are staying. He's not really my uncle, rather my father's first cousin. I call him Uncle Billy in honor of my favorite character in Frank Capra's Christmas classic, *It's a Wonderful Life*. I love how Uncle Billy—Capra's, not mine—is always slightly soused and sometimes in-the-bag hammered. The best of Uncle Billy has to be at Harry Bailey's wedding.

"I feel good enough to spit in Potter's eye! I think I will. . . . Where's my hat?"

That always cracks me up.

And when poor Uncle Billy inadvertently gives the $8,000 bank deposit to Potter, and almost single-handedly sinks the Bailey Building and Loan, he cries deep sobs of drunken despair. I get choked up every time.

My Uncle Billy and father spent a lot of time together as kids. I used to love listening to their stories about all the trouble they'd find together. When my father was just a little boy, my grandparents would put him on a train from Pittsburgh—alone, mind you—bound for New York City to visit Billy. One of my father's fondest memories is about the time he and Billy were about eight years old and spent the whole day in unaccountable bliss exploring the boroughs of New York. They started the day just monkeying around the streets of Brooklyn near Billy's home. Then, seeking new adventure, they took the train to Coney Island and hopped on a few rides. After that, the two of them rode the ferry to Staten Island to go swimming. All by themselves. A couple of eight-year-old half pints running around New York getting their kicks in the big city. However, when they returned home that night, several hours later than they were supposed to, my Great-Aunt Helen leaned out the window of their Brooklyn brownstone and cursed them to the heavens for making her worry. Wary of her wrath, they didn't want to go in the house, so they stood on the street, contemplating the severity of the beating they had coming. "We just stood there while she screamed at us," my dad recalls, breaking out in laughter at the thought of his aunt's fury.

Normally I love hearing them recall childhood shenanigans. But right now, I'm in no fucking mood. My head hurts more than usual. Way more, like I took a bath in a tub of grain alcohol and got black-out, Uncle Billy (again, Capra's, not mine) drunk through osmosis. I must be developing a tolerance to my pain medication. Every word out of their mouths feels like a dagger piercing my inner ear.

I lumber out of my bedroom grumbling, "Can you two keep it down?"

Their banter about their youth comes to an abrupt halt and I head back to my room, feeling like a dick.


Something is definitely not right. I feel even worse today than I did yesterday during my dad and uncle's head-splitting reminiscences. I didn't think that was possible. I'm also having a hard time breathing. Worse, I'm all by myself.

Gasping, I head to the bathroom, slowly raise my head, and look in the mirror. My face is swollen to twice its pre-RPG size.

*What the fuck?*

Something is definitely very wrong.

*What is it? OK. I'm having some kind of reaction. Some kind of pharmaceutical fuck up. That's obvious. OK. How do I handle this? I shuffle back to the living room, weighing my immediate future.*

*I'm all alone.*

*I am going to suffocate.*

*In this apartment.*

*Alone.*

*Get a grip. Sit.*

I plunk down on the couch, frustrated and panicked, a ripple of pain quivers in my head.

*What the hell is wrong with me?*

If I sit up straight while keeping my head down, I can breathe a little bit better. Similar to the posture you're told to assume when the plane is going down, as if lacing your fingers over your head is going to save you when you collide with the side of a mountain at 500 miles per hour.

I stay this way for more than an hour, trying not to focus on the growing tightness in my face and the thought of my head exploding like an overripe watermelon.

I hear a key in the lock. The door opens. In walks my mother. She's alone. My dad is still with Uncle Billy. He's coming over later.

"What's the matter?"

I try to calmly convey to my mother that I'm most likely asphyxiating on the rancid juices filling my head. As my mother is prone to panic, dealing with a situation like this is not her strong suit.

"What should we do?" she asks.

Good question. I hadn't thought to ask myself that until now. Sometimes a fresh perspective is best when troubleshooting a dumpster fire of a situation like this. Thanks, Mom.

I go to the notebook on the kitchen counter, the one with all the doctors' names. I start calling. It's still too early for any of them to answer their office phones. I call the hospital's emergency room and tell them my situation between labored breaths. The nurse tells me to come in right away. I call the car service I use to get around. Then we're off.

My mother guides me by the arm down the stairs and out of the building. The car arrives moments later to take us to the emergency room a few blocks away.

In the car, I curse my misfortune. Not at having been shot in the head or this morning's mysterious swelling, but the timing. Why did this have to happen with her here? She and I don't always get along, and the idea of being this scared in front of her is particularly unappealing.

When we get to the hospital, it's packed. Of course. Why wouldn't it be at 7:30 on a Wednesday morning? From best I can tell through swollen eyes, the place is riddled with battered human beings. One guy's scabby face looks like it was beat with a sock full of nickels.

I'm put in a wheelchair and taken to the back. A doctor looks me over and asks, "What's the problem?"

*Well, I currently rival the Elephant Man for most deformed head in history, but other than that I'm fine.*

"I can't breathe," I tell him between wheezes. He gives me an injection of something and a nurse runs an IV.

"It's going to be all right," says the doctor, who manages to reach one of my physicians on the phone to figure out what the hell is wrong with me. Apparently, the swelling was caused by fluid buildup from always keeping my head down. My doctors recommend that from now on I lift it for a few minutes every day so it won't, in theory, happen again.

They say I'm all right, but I don't feel all right. Far from it. I'm broken. Not just my eye and face. Everything about me is broken. My insides are shredded. I still can't figure out why she, my ex, did that to me, why our relationship fell apart, why she went from loving to loathing me.

When I start to cry my eyes swell completely shut. The tears have no place to go, filling my shuttered eyelids with salty, irritating sorrow.

"I wish he would have just killed me!" I blurt out, referring to my assailant back in Afghanistan, gripping the wheelchair's armrests and thrashing violently side to side. The chair rocks on its wheels. My mother whispers to the doctor about prescribing antidepressants, to which I am adamantly opposed.

"I won't be gorked on depression meds!" I scream out to everyone in earshot, but really I'm just addressing her.

After an hour, the swelling goes down and I'm released. My mother and I return to the apartment in silence. I go to my bedroom and close the door behind me.

# CHAPTER 16
# ZACK MORRIS IS MY LORD AND SAVIOR

OCTOBER 10, 2010
WASHINGTON HEIGHTS, NEW YORK CITY

Following doctor's orders, I raise my head for fifteen minutes a day to keep the swelling down. Dr. Schiff ensures me doing so is not jeopardizing my eye's chances of properly healing. I've been really good about keeping it down the last two weeks. Perhaps too good, he says.

Only a couple more weeks to go.

My folks returned to Pittsburgh and Franca is coming by less. I'm alone a lot, which is ideal because my disposition is not conducive to chit-chatting most days.

Social media is the limit of my engagement with the world. It provides the perfect amount of discourse, allowing me to control the flow of communication and receive in kind a flood of feigned concern from acquaintances asking how I'm doing. I tell them I'm "hanging in there," and they offer me "thoughts" and "prayers." I hear from the guys at PK that Zotto is fine. He suffered a chipped elbow and is already back. I'm almost sorry to hear that, considering a more serious injury would have gotten him out of there for good.

Some of the well wishes are from ex-girlfriends I can't believe are even talking to me. A few offer to visit. One proposes something that's particularly intriguing, though first I need to check my bank account to see if I can afford it, or at the very least put it on a credit card and worry about the consequence later.

I know I shouldn't entertain any of their offers considering the situation with Tatiana. She's been spending the occasional night here these last two weeks. We picked up where we left off before my surgery. It's been great fun, though I imagine that due to my condition our copulating is about as aerobic as still sexually active octogenarians after hip surgery.

Tatiana sometimes takes me out for some upright exercise when I need groceries. We go to a bodega down the street to pick up some essentials. As I'm in no mood to cook, I subsist on frozen pizzas, cold cuts, Ritz crackers, and peanut butter. Premium bachelor fare.

Playing over the loudspeaker in the bodega is a drum-heavy, feisty little beat from the Caribbean. Tatiana feels the rhythm in her Puerto Rican loins and does a sexy little shimmy, swinging her hips to the beat and raising her arms over her head. I lift my head even though I've already spent my fifteen minutes of head-up time today to take in the show.

"What do you think?" she says, laughing, then gives me a wink.

*I think I'm in trouble.*


Still no word from my ex. I never responded to her email telling me she was with someone else and had been for months. My current disfigurement and pain allow me to suppress thoughts of her during the day. The occasional visit by Tatiana helps too. But only in the short term.

At night, when I'm alone, I see her as I did that last time in my hotel room before the surgeries—tired, loveless eyes that wouldn't look at me before she left.

When I manage to sleep, I hear her, mocking me, telling me how much better her current fiancé is, a chronic nightmare interwoven with the rocket racing toward my head and faceless assassins coming to kill me.


Technically, meaning under no conditions whatsoever, am I supposed to venture out alone. Doctors' strictest orders. New York traffic is dangerous enough with two good eyes and your head on a swivel looking out for oncoming cars and daredevil bike couriers riding against traffic.

But the weather is turning chilly and I don't have enough warm clothing, so venture out I must to pick up some new apparel.

The prospect of going out alone scares the bejeezus out of me. It's not just my limited vision and head-down perspective of the world that has me worried. A rocket to the side of the head followed by three operations and as many weeks of near shut-in existence has rendered "outside" a scary place.

I know there is a subway station nearby. The 1 train will take me into Midtown. No harm in trying, unless I'm blindsided by the aforementioned cars and kamikaze cyclists.

I pull on that stupid roll-neck sweater Ben Plesser brought to the hospital in Germany and tape a plastic shield over my bad eye. With my head still down, per the doctors' orders (I cherry-pick which ones to follow), I slowly descend the stairs and head out the door, riddled with anxiety about what awaits me out there.

First step: Walk toward Broadway.

*This shouldn't be hard.*

No busy intersections for a couple of blocks. But my street is not without its hazards. The curb is littered with mattresses covered in blood splotches and insect carcasses. New York is in the midst of a bed-bug invasion I know all too well. Every morning I wake up covered in tiny red welts. Occasionally I squash a few between my fingers, but there are too many to make a dent in their ranks. The infestation has reached epidemic proportions in Washington Heights.

Once past the mattresses, I'm at the corner of my street and Broadway. Lots of bustle on the sidewalks and traffic in the streets. This is the scary part.

I need to get my bearings, but don't want to raise my head all the way up to read the signs. I backtrack a half dozen paces to reduce the angle of my observation. That's all the geometry I can remember from high school.

*OK. Cross the street and over one block. You can do this.*

I've seen the station's street-level railing and sign a few times coming out of the hospital. I'm pretty sure I can find it.

I'm genuinely surprised I guessed right when I arrive there. Easier than I thought.

*There aren't any boogeymen out here. Not so far. I'll keep my one good eye out for them, just in case.*

I slowly head down the stairs, go through the turnstiles, and get on a train for Midtown. I notice right away how everyone's shoes are much nicer than the desert khaki boots I'm wearing with the blood stains on the toes. The train rumbles through Harlem, down past the Upper West Side, before entering the busiest part of Manhattan. I have a couple of stops in mind.

I get off the train at 42nd Street, Times Square. Considering my visual limitations, I couldn't have picked a worse place to head-down navigate in New York. Commuters are whizzing past me left and right. I try to keep pace, but I'm afraid I'll bang into someone's back or plow into opposing pedestrians head-on. I cock my head up a few degrees so I can at least see people's butts and keep a safe distance. Sweat caused by my first real exertion in nearly a month trickles from my pits. I'm even breathing heavy. I find all this exhilarating.

*This is fantastic.*

Schiff would be really mad if he found out I was doing this. So would my editors and everyone else. It feels good to be bad.

First item on my list is a jacket. Weeks ago—while staying in the Midtown hotel where I cheated on, then lost, my fiancée—I noticed there was a Levi's store just a few blocks from my hotel. I head there and pick out a dark-blue jean jacket, the kind I had when I was 12, covered with buttons advertising my affinity for British teen angst bands like The Smiths and Depeche Mode. I have been looking for an excuse to buy another one. When I try it on, I can feel the sales clerks eye me suspiciously. I can't blame them. A bearded weirdo walks into your store trying on jean jackets and refusing to raise his head is going to get some side glances. I amble to the counter with my purchase, pull out a credit card, and buy the jacket. Money makes people overlook all kinds of oddities.

Next, the headwear. This is something I'd given some thought while I've been laid up. I want something spiffy, though functional. Something that will keep me warm and convey a little cool. I'm not much of a fashionista, but under the circumstances I figure I'll treat myself. I arrive at the place I previously scoped online for headwear: JJ's Hats on Fifth Avenue in the shadow of the Empire State Building. They specialize in wool, flat-brim caps. Growing up in Pittsburgh, where a large number of Italians settled at the turn of the 20th century, I'd seen plenty of old guys wearing those hats. I always thought they were cool. I just needed an excuse to buy one. I pick a brown tweed one from the case and place it on my head, angling the brim so it shades my bad eye.

When I lift my head up all the way to check myself out in a mirror, I laugh. I imagine I look like a reasonable approximation of my great-grandfather, fresh off the boat at Ellis Island, raring to hit the big city and get his head kicked in while pursuing The American Dream.

*Giovanni Gentile would approve.*

I'm staring at this box in my living room that arrived more than two weeks ago. It came by delivery, DHL, all the way from Afghanistan. About a week after my surgery, the intercom buzzed and a voice said he had a delivery for me. Not expecting a package, I was shocked by its size and heft. Two men had lugged it up three flights of stairs with some apparent difficulty—I heard them grunting and huffing before they knocked on my door.

When I answer, they're standing behind an olive drab container made of a composite plastic, a model I've seen at the foot of soldiers' bunks.

The label reads:

**CAPT. ALEX TORRES**
**1–32 CAVALRY**
**FOB BOSTICK**
**APO AE0931**

**PERSONAL EFFECTS: GENTILE, CARMEN**
**ATT: SGT CHRISTINA M. DION**
**CJTF - 101 PAO 300TH MPAD**
**APO AE 09354**

I can guess what's in it. Presumably it's everything I had with me when I got shot, plus all my gear that was scattered on and around my bunk at PK. I should be glad to have it. But I'm not. There are boogeymen in that box. Mean-spirited, ill-tempered, out-to-get-me war goblins are in that box. I'm already having a hard enough time coping with what happened to me. I don't need what's in there kicking my anxiety into high gear.

My fear of facing what's in that box is what keeps me from investigating anything Afghanistan-related. I haven't read a single story out of the country since I was hurt. Uncle Billy brought me a copy of Sebastian Junger's new book, *War*, about an outpost of soldiers in Afghanistan and the challenges they face. I had asked him to buy it for me. I haven't so much as cracked the cover. I just can't.

I promised my editors at *USA Today* that I would write a story about PK and what happened to me there. But I'm not sure I can. Besides, my laptop and all my expensive gear—the cameras I was carrying when I got hit, my helmet, body armor, everything—was either taken from me by invisible hands while being treated or left behind. It might be in that box. Perhaps worse, it's not and I'm out a lot of expensive stuff. If it isn't, do I go out and buy all new things? It might not be worth it. Lately, I've been thinking I may never report again. Questions about my career lead to long bouts of staring into the existential abyss: How did I wind up in this sorrowful state? What am I going to do now? Will I ever work as a journalist again?

Confusion about one's place in the universe is apparently the norm when you stare at the floor all the time. But now I'm standing next to the box, so I'm staring at it. Every day I do this. Every day I stare at this box and say, "This is the day I'm going to open you!"

But I never do. Over these past two weeks, that box taunting me every time I walk past it.

Till today.

*Today is the day, you motherfucker.*

*It has to be someday, and today is as good a day as any.*

I take a deep breath, then let it out, just like I did with that catheter nurse I whizzed on, recalling how much I enjoyed that.

*OK, you can do this. Let's go. Just open the damn box.*

I take a step back and circle around the living room.

*Come on!*

I walk back up to the box and start flipping open the plastic latches, two on the front, two on each side. The release of each clasp makes my heart skip.

My hands find the edges of the lid. This is it.

*Ready . . .*

*Set . . .*

*Go.*

I throw open the box and am immediately blown backwards.

"Holy fuck, that stinks!"

An invisible, toxic miasma of my own body odor and a collection of scents from the bowels of PK smacks me square in my still-tender face and I'm immediately transported back to that tiny combat outpost. On top is the crusty collection of well-worn socks I'd stashed beneath my bunk. I was on the fence about throwing those things in the burn pit while at PK. Now that they've had a few weeks to marinate, they really have to go. I grab the lot of them and toss them in the kitchen garbage can. I can still smell them under the sink with the cabinet door closed.

What remains are essentials: my passport, tucked neatly in the corner of the box so as not to be fouled by the rest of my gear, and my laptop, battered by weeks of abuse in the dusty Kandahar Desert before Kunar. The battery is dead. At first I'm afraid it might be toast, considering the asthmatic sputtering sound the fan was making even before I was shot. I dig out the power cord and plug it in. After a tense moment of silence, the laptop flashes to life with its unmistakable MacBook *Boooong!* At least I won't have to buy a new one.

The rest of my gear is wedged into the case chaotically, denoting the quickness with which it was likely packed after my injury. Sweat-stained T-shirts are wrapped around my still-photo camera, a dozen cables for connecting cameras to my laptop or my laptop to my audio recorder and video camera are tangled in a ball like Clark Griswold's Christmas lights. I spot my helmet, covered in a Rorschach of dried blood stains, and an old pair of leather boots with one sole separated from the upper. No sign of my body armor, however. My first thought is that someone swiped it because the plates alone cost a couple thousand bucks. Then it occurs to me that clothing saturated with blood is burned by the military as a biological hazard.

*Damn.*

That's going to take a real bite out of my wallet. I loved that vest, with its slick zip-up-the-front style and body-hugging design. I looked positively gangster in that thing.

I sort through the rest of my gear, pulling out more clothes and my camera bag till I reach the bottom of the box. There, battered and abused, its microphone hanging precariously by a length of cord tied to the handle, is my video camera—the camera I was filming with when I was shot. I'm not sure it works anymore. I did drop the thing when I got hit. But there's a chance I caught the attack right up to the point where I was shot in the head.

I backtrack through the moment before impact like I have countless times in my waking nightmares. Except this time, I'm looking for clues. I was pointing my camera at those young men on the side of the road. Then I whipped around to see the rocket heading right toward me.

*Maybe I did catch it. Maybe the worst fucking moment of my life is captured on this camera.*

Though everything else that was in the box is now scattered around the living room, I decide to put the camera back inside it.

I'm not ready to find out what's on there.


Every morning before dawn it's the same routine. I shuffle to the living room and ease myself into my massage chair, carefully inserting my pumpkin-sized, bearded face into the chair's padded donut to watch "the gang" through a mirror pointed at the TV.

One of the only reasons I bother to get out of bed is so I can watch my new favorite show. Since the start of my head-down convalescence, I've developed an unhealthy affinity for *Saved by the Bell*, which airs for two hours every morning starting at six. There is something alluring about Lisa Turtle's pastel, off-the-shoulder sweatshirts and sassy attitude. Zack Morris's acid-washed jeans and bleached-blond hair helmet ooze high school cool and Iran Contra–era panache. Even the shrill voice of Screech Powers is soothing after yet another night of neck-aching, sporadic slumber caused by that stupid fucking donut pillow. I'm enthralled by the sweet-and-sour romance of Bayside's half-shirted, mullet-king, AC Slater, and his nerdy, horsey-faced girlfriend (later turned real-life, semi–soft-core porn actress) Jessie Spano as they spend prom night trapped in the school boiler room dancing to the music trickling through the vents and proclaiming their affections for one another after yet another all-out screaming match.

*When will those two ever come to terms with their love?*

And when Zack and Kelly finally tie the knot in Vegas following a series of misfortunes involving a Native American mechanic with killer abs and something about Mr. Morris becoming a gigolo (that part I might have hallucinated), I tear up ever so slightly, mourning an end to friendships that have come to mean so much to me.

That is, until doctors cut off my supply of OxyContin. With no more opiates on which to watch my newfound favorite show, the gang from Bayside quickly loses its appeal.

As sad as the loss of my affinity for the Bayside gang may be, there is an even more troubling matter brewing in my no-longer-numbed skull, a concern bubbling from the deep recess of a semi-lucid mind.

Namely, is this it for me? Is this all I have to look forward to for the rest of my miserable life? I've already spent several weeks physically and mentally atrophying in front of the TV and my laptop. The average American supposedly watches about six hours of television a day. I'm doubling that these days, easily.

Last month I was hiking mountains in Afghanistan. Now I get winded when I walk to the bathroom. Worse, if I'm permanently debilitated—say, blind in one eye—then I might not be able to do lots of things I love. Can I surf with only one eye? Without decent depth perception, judging the size and distance of approaching waves might make riding them impossible. What about my motorcycle? Can I ride my bike if I can't check my right-hand mirror or accurately gauge the distance between me and other vehicles?

I shudder to think of the potential losses I hadn't contemplated till now. Surfing and riding are the twin pillars of my being. Not being able to do these things would be an even bigger bummer than losing touch with my pals from Bayside.


There's another problem plaguing me, one that I haven't discussed with my doctors or anyone else due to my unusual embarrassment. Because opiates make their users constipated, I haven't pooped for weeks. I've got a boulder-size blockage residing in my gut.

I thought about this from time to time while riding my narcotic high, but couldn't be bothered to do anything about it. Now that I'm off the meds, and still nothing's happening, I'm more than a little worried. My belly feels like Cool Hand Luke's after he's eaten all those eggs. It's so taut and distended the only pants I can wear are the PJs with the drawstring. I've started waddling when I walk, like all the old men in my family. I hand Franca a piece of paper with the words "stool softener" written in block letters and ask her to take it to the nearest pharmacy.

She returns a half hour later with a small bottle. The instructions say take two. I swallow three for good measure, reasoning that the creators of this particular laxative have never had the misfortune of being shot in the face and had to ingest enough OxyContin to constipate an elephant. After a while, I feel a faint rumbling in my gut. I haven't heard a peep out of my nether region in so long that I'm startled. This is it. Showtime.

But when I try to get the ball rolling, the obstruction proves too great. Sitting on the toilet, I try to force the matter, wedging my left hand under the rim of the nearby sink and placing the other on the towel rack to get a better grip.

"Huhhhhhhhh!"

Nothing going. The blockage it so persistent I can feel the pressure from pushing all the way up into my head and face. I try again and remind myself to not hold my breath for fear I might pass out.

"Huhhhhhhhhhhhhhhhh!"

Nope. That time made my eye hurt. That's all I need—explain to Schiff and the rest of the doctors that I undid all their fancy doctoring by popping out my surgically repaired eye while desperately trying to take a dump.

*This is not happening. I'm not going back to the hospital to have some poor nurse stick yet another finger in my rectum to dis-impact me.*

Then I remember something I read about a yoga position that lines up the bowels. Where did I see that? *Cosmo?* I used to read it all the time when I was a lifeguard in college. It was always around.

Amazed I recalled a factoid in a women's magazine from fifteen years ago, I begin to strategize the extraction. First, I get in the tub. If this is going to be as gross as I think it is, best to keep the disaster contained. Then I get into downward facing dog, or whatever the hell it's called when you're prone on all fours. Head down, ass up. Then, breathe. In through the nose, out through the mouth, or something like that. Or is it in and out through the nose? I don't know. Yoga is dumb. But I'm desperate.

*Just relax. Breathe however you want.*

Not sure whether what happens next is attributable to the yoga pose or the high-grade poop shoot cleanser Franca bought, but the train begins to ever so slowly leave the station. The girth of the mass trying to make its way out of me is startling.

*What the fuck?*

I feel like I'm being ripped open by two backhoes digging a swimming pool in opposite directions. My eyes water like facets open full bore. I'm covered in flop sweat. I need to end this quickly. I reach around and grab ahold of what's peeking out of me. I feel like it's the girth of a soda can. One good push oughta do it. Then I can get a proper grip on it and guide the rest out.

*Here we go.*

Of all the unseemly sounds I've emitted in the course of my unfortunate brush with that Taliban rocket, the wail I emit while pulling a foot and a half of feces out of my own rectum is by far the most primal. It's reminiscent of the legendary wailing of a gut-stabbed Grendel when slain by Beowulf. Epic verse should be written about my howling, which rattles the sides of the steel tub I'm in as well as the building's iron girders.

I place the extracted obstruction in the commode—I'm quite certain it won't be disposed of in fewer than a dozen flushes—then lie back in the tub, completely spent. My belly slowly returns to normal as I momentarily bask in the simple joy of clear bowels and await the inevitable onset of crippling humiliation.

My bad dreams persist. They are a mash of horrorscapes, always ending in my death. Over the last few weeks, I've been shot by a firing squad, burned alive while cuffed to a chain-link fence, and, of course, repeatedly hit with a rocket that almost always decapitates me. Sometimes I have the pleasure of surviving my beheading for a short while, my head lying on its side, and watching as my twitching body slowly goes limp. When I wake up I'm clenching my fists so tightly that I've lost all circulation in my hands. My fingers ache when I try to relax them. I need to either bash myself over the head with the business end of a hammer to make these dreams stop or get some help.

I tell my nurse case manager, Rosa Stagnitta—she handles all the appointments for my various physicians—to book me an appointment with a psychiatrist. Maybe I can figure out how I can make these dreadful visions go away. And since the insurance company for CBS is paying for it, I might as well get my head shrunk on their dime.

Dr. David Schlugar has a Park Avenue office on the ground floor of one of those old New York apartment buildings with a doorman who wears frilly epaulets and a cap with a patent leather brim. He blocks my entrance while asking me where I'm going. I tell him "Schlugar's" while trying to avoid eye contact. I'm not crazy about telling a stranger I'm here for psychiatric help. He moves aside and tells me where to go. I knock at the doctor's door and Schlugar himself answers, then shows me to his office where he offers me a seat in a large, leather wingback chair reminiscent of those found on the set of *Masterpiece Theatre* next to a roaring fire. The good doctor and I exchange a handful of pleasantries, then it's off to the races.

"What can I do for you?"

I tell him what happened to me, not sure how much he knows. He doesn't give any indication that he's familiar with my injury, my work, anything about me. Psychiatrists generally like to let patients tell their stories in their own words. My story is full of expletives. Lots of them. F-bombs are flying out of my mouth at a staccato pace. I'm wondering if he can even understand what I'm saying when I notice he picks up on my speech patterns and word usage and parrots them back to me. I think he's trying to foster feelings of camaraderie. Under normal circumstances, I would find this annoying and contrived. But in my current condition, it is exactly what I need: someone on my side.

"It's just so fucked," I say, punctuating an outburst about my injury.

"That is fucked," he agrees.

I tell him that despite my rage and nightmares I hope I can return to Afghanistan when I'm well, that my feelings about what happened to me are often in conflict with one another. I tell him I even sort of feel bad for the guy who shot me. Imagine having to explain that fuck-up to your fellow Taliban fighters. "Did you hear what happened to Abdullah? Dummy forgot to arm the rocket and it hit one of the Americans in the head. Didn't even kill him. What a fucking moron!"

With my head down, I can't see Schlugar's reaction to anything I'm telling him: the RPG, the surgery, my bad dreams, fears about my future. And of course, my ex. I talk about her a lot, about how much she hurt me. She hasn't contacted me since sending the email telling me she was in love with someone else.

"Then she rubs it in my fucking face that she's fucking someone else? Who the fuck does that?"

By the time I'm done unburdening myself, I'm nearly out of breath. Schlugar remains silent. I can see from the top of my good eye his hands are folded under his chin. Then, after a beat, he offers his assessment.

"She sounds like a bitch."

*I like this guy.*

# CHAPTER 17
# AN "ACCIDENTAL" PROFESSION OF LOVE
NOVEMBER, 27, 2009
JUPITER, FLORIDA

*I hate doing these kinds of stories.*

*It's not that I think they are beneath me . . . but they totally are.*

The *New York Times* called me this morning to report on a multiple homicide in Jupiter, the victims of which include a six-year-old girl. While suburban murder sprees are not usual fare for *Times* coverage, those on Thanksgiving in South Florida make the cut because traditionally it's a slow news day and the editors in New York love stories that allow them to look down their collective noses at this part of the country and its ass-backward inhabitants from their lofty, erudite perch in Manhattan. I'm no better, what with my own sneering at this story. After two months in Afghanistan covering firefights and the finer points of an ongoing conflict where millions of lives are at stake, I'm back in the states covering a holiday homicide, which brings me in closer proximity to more dead bodies than I had been the whole two-and-a-half months I was in Afghanistan this last go around.

*What the fuck is wrong with this country?*

My crankiness is not just seeded in having to cover this particular story. I'm especially displeased about standing outside a crime scene blocked off by police tape because I just got back to Miami yesterday and want to spend every moment with my lovely new federal agent girlfriend. My only consolation is that she's celebrating the holiday with her family. I had been looking forward to catching up on some much-needed sleep and dozing beside her this morning when I received the call to come up here and cover this. So instead of languishing in bed with her, I ride my motorcycle 89 miles north to this crime scene, leaving my lovely behind in my new apartment, a tiny studio I rented near the beach that she and I quickly made our universe.

We've picked up right where we left off before I went to Afghanistan, having all but consumed one another since I've been back. When we aren't satiating our beastly needs, we talk at length about the efficacy of the surge strategy in Afghanistan and what she can disclose about her own work. While I was away she'd had a couple of high-profile assignments looking after foreign diplomats, the scant details of which I couldn't get enough. We're talking world leaders. Big ones. Her work fascinates me and I gobble up what scraps she can disclose. Bodyguard duty, the occasional undercover assignment requiring a bit of acting and costumes. It's all so . . . sexy.

It's only been a few hours since we parted this morning, but the signs of withdrawal are apparent and painful. I sigh like a schoolgirl when thinking about her.

"Hey baby," she says when she answers my call. "What are you doing?"

"Nothing much. Just standing here waiting to hear something about these dead people."

"I miss you. It's crazy how much I miss you." Her voice is tender and full of longing.

"You too. I'll come back as soon as I'm done here. Will I see you tonight?"

"I hope. Tomorrow at the latest. I have to work."

"Ugh. I can't wait that long," I tell her.

"I know. Me neither."

"Go be with your family. I'll finish up here and race back on the chance you can stay over tonight," I tell her.

"OK. Sounds good. I'll see you soon. Love you . . . "

. . . .

. . . .

"Wait . . . I . . . ummm . . . woah . . . that just came out."

"It's OK," I say laughing. "I know the feeling."

After filing my story, I race back to Miami to be with her. That night we sprawl out on my bed.

Her soft brown locks are splayed out on the bed, her eyes seem slightly teary.

"Are we going to talk about it?" I ask.

"What?" she says feigning confusion.

"You know."

"I know. I don't . . . I'm sorry if I said . . . I didn't mean to . . . I don't know."

"I love you too."

# CHAPTER 18
# A CYCLOPS AND CRANBERRY SAUCE

NOVEMBER, 25, 2010
PITTSBURGH, PENNSYLVANIA

Thomas is looking at me quizzically without saying a word, which is unusual considering my eight-year-old nephew is not shy about speaking his mind. My arrival at my sister's home in Pittsburgh for Thanksgiving marks the first time Tara and her two boys have seen me since my injury. When I walk in the door, she greets me as if nothing has happened, offering her usual, "Hey, Carmen." I reply similarly. We've probably exchanged no more than a 100 words in the last decade. There's no acrimony between us; we just don't have much to say to each other.

Frankie, her youngest, asks lots of questions about the war, what happened to me, and whether my experiences bear any resemblance to the first-person warfare video games he and his brother play.

"If your head gets blown off, you die," Frankie, who is all of six, informs me with gleeful exuberance, as if he were telling me about what he hoped Santa would bring him.

"Good to know. I appreciate the tip."

I was cleared to raise my head just a few days ago, though I'm not out of the woods yet. I still have regular checkups and another surgery in a few months.

Getting out of that Washington Heights apartment that's been the scene of so much existential malaise it could be the setting of a Samuel Beckett play was a good move, though I'm still a train wreck of a human being.

The hurt inflicted on me by both my ex-fiancée and the Taliban is sticking around despite my best efforts to hump it a way with Tatiana. Their ranking flip-flops day to day. I'm still having the death dreams. Repeat visits to Schlugar's office to vent have reduced their frequency and severity. But every few days another nasty one manifests, causing me to flail myself awake drenched in sweat. During the day, my feelings of rejection and inadequacy in the face of my one-time fiancée are manifest more frequently now that I don't have my pain meds. Tatiana's voraciousness in the sack helps, but not as well as I hoped.

Due to my current state, I've largely kept to myself since I got home a couple of days ago. I don't feel like seeing anyone. My folks told me to call so-and-so and go see one of their friends who'd been asking about me. But I didn't. The only person I really wanted to see while I'm here is my grandma, who couldn't make the trip to New York. Despite her frailty, she remains sharp and wise. I've always relied on her for her no-nonsense, yet compassionate, counsel. She's the only person in my family with whom I feel comfortable talking about personal matters. Years earlier, when I was going through another breakup with yet another who professed to love me despite reconciling with her ex-boyfriend right under my nose, she listened to me blubber, then offered a stark, thoughtful assessment of the woman's actions:

"Love is in the doing, not the saying."

Her wisdom then obviously applies to my current situation. Yet she resists reminding me. She could tell when I walked in the door I was in no mood to talk about my ex.

Sitting at her kitchen table over coffee, we instead talked about my nephews, the upcoming holiday, and my work. I told her I wanted to go back to Afghanistan. I'm not a hundred percent sure I do, but the urge to return is growing each day even though the very idea of setting foot in Afghanistan still panics me to the point of hysteria.

Before now, I'd only mulled over returning to Afghanistan privately. I couldn't tell my parents this. They'd lose their minds. Same with friends. But my grandma, who'd grown up impoverished during the height of the Depression, spent part of her childhood in an orphanage, endured two terrible marriages and her own bout of lost eyesight due to macular degeneration, knows something about enduring hard times and possesses a stubborn streak that would put your average pack mule to shame. It's a trait we share. When I finish confessing my desire to go back she sits quietly, then offers an anecdote in response.

"You know, when I was a girl, there was a reporter on the news reels who wore an eyepatch."

She tells me about the heroic and gallant newspaper and radio reporter Floyd Gibbons who lost his eye during World War I while covering the fighting in France. When she was a girl, and on the rare occasion could afford a movie ticket, she saw Gibbons on the screen, a white patch over his left socket, reporting the leading events of the day.

When I get up to leave, I lean over so she can wrap her frail arms around my neck. She tells me she loves me and expresses her giddiness about seeing my nephews at Thanksgiving in a couple of days.

"I'm so proud of you," she says. "You know, I was so worried when your mother told me what happened. I said 'Oh no, he's so handsome!'" She looks me over with her own infirmed eyes.

"You are still very handsome."


After Thanksgiving dinner, the boys and I sit on the floor to play with their LEGOS, which were my LEGOS when I was their age. Apparently, my parents have no hope that I'll procreate, so many of my childhood mementos have been passed on to them. Worse yet, my entire collection of *Star Wars* figures went to some other unrelated kids, never to be seen again.

*How I long for you, Hoth Planet Han Solo in your dashing winter wear suited for subzero Tauntaun riding.*

Thomas looks up from the spaceship we're building and stares deeply into my bad eye. "Uncle Carmen, you look like a Cyclops."

I know I'm expected to laugh off his unfiltered observation as the product of youth still unfamiliar with the finer points of social constraint and decorum.

But I'm really tempted to tell him there's no Santa Claus.

# PART TWO

See, everybody else looks out at the world through both eyes.
But I only need one eye for that. With the other, I'm able to look
inside, see what nobody else can see.

—Floyd Gibbons, as portrayed by
Scott Brady in the TV series *The Untouchables*

Myself and the company commander at Pirtle King, along with an Afghan commander and local from a nearby village. *(Credit for all photos: Carmen Gentile.)*

This is the last known picture of me with two good eyes. Late summer 2010, Kandahar Province. Check out all the weed behind me.

Combat Outpost Pirtle King in Kunar Province is surrounded by mountains on all sides, making it an ideal target for the Taliban.

A plaque at Combat Outpost Pirtle King in dedication to the fallen soldiers for which it was named.

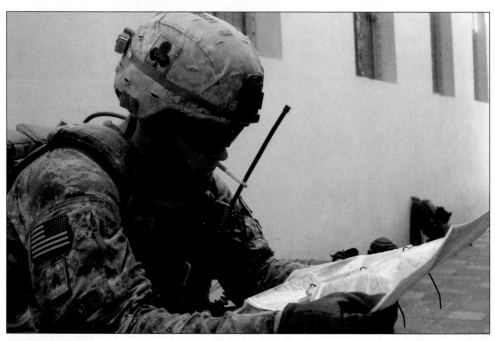
Sgt. Grant Aaron Thomson, who bandaged me after I was hit, consults a map in Kunar Province a few days before the attack.

Moments after I'm injured, Sgt. Grant Aaron Thomson treats my injury, while others tend to Lt. Derek Zotto (right) lying on the ground.

Sgt. Grant Aaron Thomson wraps a bandage around my head just moments after being hit with a rocket-propelled grenade.

The view from a Blackhawk helicopter over southern Afghanistan.

Soldiers at Combat Outpost Pirtle King return fire with mortars amid a Taliban attack, summer 2012.

An Afghan National Army soldier examines his bunk after a Taliban attack at Pirtle King left it riddled with bullet and shrapnel holes.

Soldiers with the Afghan National Army live in spartan barracks with few amenities.

Teenage members of the Afghan Local Police.

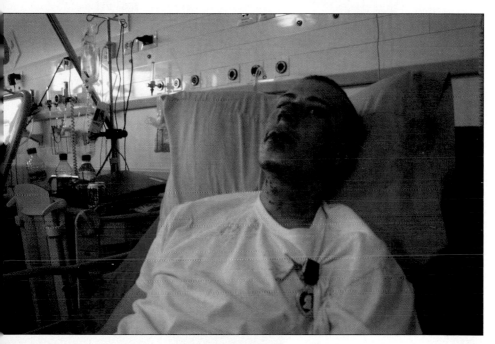

Spc. Joshua Pederson recovers in an Army hospital in Kandahar Airfield after his armored vehicle came under Taliban attack, injuring his eyes and face.

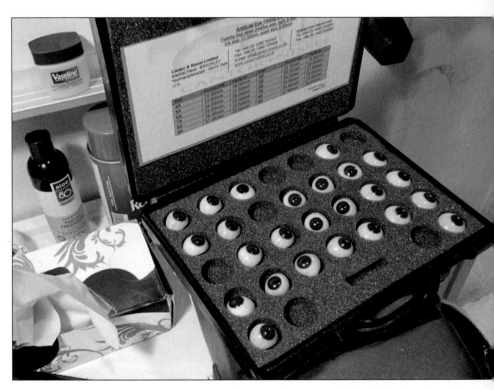

A selection of prosthetic eyes at the military hospital at Bagram Airfield, where an opthomologist was able to save my eye after I was shot in Kunar.

A soldier from Combat Outpost Honaker Miracle.

A Marine's below-ground barracks at Patrol Base Shark's Tooth.

Some Marines at Patrol Base Shark's Tooth live outdoors in the scorching summer heat.

Senators Liebermann, McCain, and Graham at Bagram Airfield on the Fourth of July.

American soldiers patrol past the wreckage of Soviet armored vehicles in a remote corner of Ghazni Province, winter 2012.

Me working on the first draft of *Blindsided by the Taliban* in January 2014.

# CHAPTER 19
# A RING OF TRUTH

JANUARY 5, 2011
WASHINGTON, DC

*I shouldn't be here.*

Not in this Washington, DC, hotel, where I've been holed up the last three days surrounded by the assorted detritus of my on-the-go, hobo lifestyle: a half-eaten container of General Tso's chicken; dozens of receipts from months of taxis, trains, and planes; the engagement ring I gave my ex just over a year ago.

*Not here, here. "Here," with the big "H." On this earth. Among the living.*

The founding tenets of probability dictate, in no uncertain terms, that I should not be alive after getting shot in the head with a rocket-propelled grenade. It just doesn't make sense. I've run through the attack countless times, masochistically pouring over each moment, starting when I first notice the eyes of the Afghan men widen, then turn to see what caught their attention, recognize the weapon on the man's shoulder, the trail of smoke, the conical tip and the rocket's impact on my face. Every time I'm hit, my whole body shudders as if I'm having a micro seizure. This is happening all the time now, whether I'm walking down the street, lying in bed alone, or with someone else, anywhere. These little fits jostle me from my remembrance of that small village in Kunar and I wake up "Here," feeling like I don't belong because I should not exist.

There's a lot of self-inflicted mind play at work here, I know that. But I can't seem to logic my way out of this loop of self-indulgent, perpetual-negation bullshit. Deep down I know I should be giggling like an idiot every moment of every day while prancing through the streets with joy and gratitude pouring from my heart. But I can't seem to get there. I'm not thankful.

But I do feel guilty for not being thankful, for not celebrating every moment of my now improbable existence.

That's really the worst part about surviving the closest of close calls: dealing with the guilt of not constantly being grateful. I just don't see how. The residue of that one harrowing moment sticks to everything else in my life. Every subsequent experience is infected by near death, a constant reminder of how close I was to not being "Here."

A banging on the door interrupts this near-perpetual stream of self-involvement. The same cleaning lady with the ear-piercing falsetto knocks every day around this time. When she does, I'm always lying in bed grinding through the same ole' existential angst that never gets resolved.

"Sir. Sir! You need towel?"

*No, I don't need towel. I need something I can't quite figure out, though I doubt it's on your housekeeping cart.*

*

I'm still jet-lagged from my trip to Australia and New Zealand though I've been back for weeks. At least that's what I tell myself to justify spending day and night in bed watching bad TV.

*You just need to rest up.*

I tell myself the whirlwind pace I kept Down Under still has me tuckered out and that it has nothing to do with the fact that I've been dreading coming back to Washington to have my guts kicked out.

While planning my trip, I was excited, even happy. I first started scheming it while I was house-bound and head-down in New York. The idea of a getting away to the other side of the planet was the only thing that gave me pleasure. That, and the occasional romp with Tatiana.

I told Tatiana I needed a much-needed break from the invasive surgeries and post-op probing. She thought it was a great idea, though said she'll miss me while I'm gone, which I pretended not to hear when we say our goodbyes.

"Hmmm? What's that? OK . . . See you."

"Have fun, dick. And be careful," she tells me moments before I boarded my flight for Sydney.

I assured Tatiana I would, just as I did Dr. Schiff, who during my last examination said it was OK for me to go as long as I took it easy. I told him not to worry. I wouldn't do anything to jeopardize his and the other doctors' handiwork.

I, of course, was lying and broke those promises almost immediately upon arrival in Australia. There's no way I'd travel all that way and not at the very least surf the legendary Bondi Beach. Despite the risk, I was determined to test my now distorted depth perception against the rising swell of five-foot waves to see if I could still ride. The prognosis initially looked grim. After repeatedly falling ass over ears into the frothing white water, I started to worry my surfing days were behind me for good.

Then, with my bad eye shut tight, I finally figured out how to adjust my timing to my new view of the oceanic horizon. When the next wave approached, I paddled into it until I felt the board match the wave's momentum, then popped up to my feet. Aligned with the transcendent groove of the cresting waters, I carved up and down the face and bellowed a caterwauling "Whooooooooooooo!"

Having caught my first post-Taliban-RPG wave, I felt like I could do anything, like, say, go free diving on the Great Barrier Reef, another Dr. Schiff–ordered no-no. He said specifically that diving would put too much pressure on my surgically repaired peeper. But I did it anyway and came away no worse for wear.

Invigorated by my defiance, I decided it was time to add some speed to the trip, so when I reached New Zealand I rented an off-road motorbike to take on some backwoods trails. My yen for adrenaline however caught up with me when I wiped out on a sharp, banked turn, leaving me with a gnarly purple-and-yellow bruise on my right thigh. After that I dialed back the intensity a bit, opting for a whitewater rafting tour, then rounded out my journey with a day-long trek along the face of a glacier.

Was I carelessly endangering my still-recovering face and eye? Oh yeah. But it was the first time I felt normal in months. And to me, even though it would only last a little while, it was worth the risk.

When not breaking promises to my doctors and ambiguous sex partner that I'd be careful, I was pulling another stunt Down Under that would have particularly peeved Tatiana.

I didn't exactly go on my trip alone, as I might have implied to her, or perhaps even outright stated, in the weeks leading up to my departure. Truth was, I had a companion, a female companion. And not just any female companion, but an exquisite one: my ex-girlfriend Fernanda from when I lived in Rio de Janeiro. A scalding temptress and extraordinary woman with whom I had once been crazy in love, Fernanda reached out to me soon after I was shot. Even though our relationship had ended years earlier on bad terms (mostly my fault), she'd expressed heartfelt concern about my physical and emotional well-being at a time I was particularly vulnerable to the doting of sympathetic women who wanted to have sex.

So, at the same time Tatiana was helping soothe my physical injuries and broken heart, I kind of, sort of, rekindled my relationship with Fernanda and arranged to travel with her in Australia and New Zealand right under Tatiana's nose.

I justified the deception by telling myself I was "owed" this adventure with a woman I once loved and that our shared history trumped the new and undefined connection Tatiana and I developed in the days after I was shot.

The trip was chocked with emotional extremes that rivaled my adventuring in their intensity. During our travels Fernanda and I either copulated furiously and romanticized our past, or screamed at one another while relitigating those arguments that lead to our breakup five years earlier. By the end, we were both emotionally raw from the experience.

"I thought maybe we would spend all this time together and you would fall in love with me again," she said at the end of three weeks of close proximity. In hindsight, it was probably not the smartest idea, considering how long it had been since we'd last seen each other.

On that rainy last day in Auckland, sitting on a bench overlooking the harbor, her vulnerable admission made me tear up. I stared at the face of a lovely woman deserving so much to be loved and searched for the feelings I once had for her. I told myself I should be in love with Fernanda.

But I was not in love with Fernanda. Maybe I should have been in love with Tatiana, who nurtured me when I was at my facially disfigured worst following my operation, and had been sending me emails about a "surprise" when I get back.

But I was not in love with her either.

Though loathe to admit it, I was, inexplicably and quite unfortunately, still in love with my ex.

It's not as if I never get out of bed now. Why just moments ago I was upright and outside, willingly enduring the biting January cold. The tip of my nose still feels frosty as I lie here in my underwear with the heat cranked up to 80.

My ex and I had arranged to meet in my hotel's lobby not fifteen minutes ago so she could give the engagement ring back to me. When I arrived downstairs she's already there, bundled in a bulky parka I've never seen her wear, as most of our courtship was relegated to sunny South Florida.

She mustered a faint "Hey" when I entered the lobby. I shrugged my shoulders, then suggested we go outside and sit in her car rather than conduct our impromptu un-engagement ceremony in a lobby full of strangers.

We sat in her silver Miata, shivering, each of us trying to figure out what was worth saying, if anything.

She looked me over.

"It's not bad," she said of my eye, which is especially red and irritated today due to the cold and wind.

I stared straight ahead while seated in the passenger seat, uncertain of the protocol for reacquiring an engagement ring. But before I can ask for it, my ex had a request of her own.

"Oh, can you write me a check for the storage space? Your end comes out to $200," she informed me, having decided that I should pay for more of it because my boxes of books and clothes—which were supposed to one day be in a home we share—take up more space than her stuff.

"I'll write you a check," I told her.

With nothing else to distract us from the task at hand, she dug through her purse for the black box containing the engagement ring I gave her last year when she came to Pittsburgh to meet my family. She handed it to me and I stared at it for a moment, then started saying something I already regretted midsentence.

"I can't . . . I can't do this," she said interrupting me, staring straight ahead, gripping the wheel tightly as if steering the parked car required all her concentration.

A deep hurt swelled in my belly. I turned away so as not to show her the pained look on my face. I got out of the car and watched her pull away, turn left onto 14th Street, and disappear.

# CHAPTER 20
# IS THE TIMING RIGHT?

JANUARY 1, 2010
PITTSBURGH, PENNSYLVANIA

*This has to be perfect.*
*Not for me, but for her.*
*She'll be telling this story of how I did it for decades to come.*
*I've got to do this just right.*
*What's the clothing protocol?*
*Can we be naked for this?*
*Is that somehow disrespectful?*
*I think it's romantic.*

She and I have been talking about our future all morning, about how we want to spend our lives together seeing the world and sharing adventures. How we've each found the one that makes the other want to share everything. This is well-trodden ground for us, even though we've been together a short time. She's probably going to be transferred one day to work at an American embassy. It won't be in Paris, she assures me. First foreign postings are usually "hardship" assignments. Someplace more like Chad or Mozambique. I tell her it doesn't matter to me. I can work from pretty much anywhere. Besides, my career will once again become a secondary concern, just as it should be.

*This is the right time.*
*I'm just going to do it.*

My heart is pounding harder than it ever has. She notices and puts a hand on my chest.

"What is it, baby?"

Reaching into the drawer next to the bed, I pull out the small box I placed there yesterday.

"Will you maa-marry me?" I ask, stammering through the most important question of my life.

She sits up, the bedsheet falling from her naked torso, and stares at the ring in the box.

"Yes."

I slip the ring on her finger. It's a little loose. "We'll get it sized," I tell her with a nervous laugh. Her acceptance feels tenuous to me.

Then she says:

"Oh my God, we're getting married!"

*That's better.*

# CHAPTER 21
# CANNONBALL RUN

JANUARY 6, 2011
ARLINGTON, VIRGINIA

I pull off the tarp and snow fills the air.

*Hello, my darling. I've missed you.*

*You are right to be mad. I've sorely neglected you these last five months since you carried me here on what I thought was my final migration north to join my ex.*

*Sorry I made you wait here, in the cold, for nothing.*

Her chain is embarrassingly rusty; the links appear welded together by dampness and neglect. A friend was supposed to start her for me every once in a while. I think he may have a few times. "But it's been a while," he admitted.

I'm not sure he ever took her out. His wife frowns on him riding, even though he used to have one. I can't blame him or her.

*I'm sorry, baby. This is all my fault.*

I run my hand over Lucille—I named my motorcycle after the prick-teasing, car-washing seductress in *Cool Hand Luke*—and inspect the rest of her.

*No worse for wear.*

Actually, she's in pretty sorry shape. Besides spending months outside with no one riding her, only a thin tarp protecting her from the snow and other elements, Lucille is battered and bruised. Her tank panels are scratched from when I laid her down on a backwoods trail in the Everglades, the lettering denoting her as a BMW "Dakar" is peeling off. The right-side mirror is gone, broken off when I dropped her at a dead stop on a slight incline in the parking lot of my old apartment building. That didn't stop me from riding her all the way north with only one mirror. Incredibly dangerous and illegal. But now that I can't see out of my right eye, it seems silly to put off leaving to replace it. I want to get the hell out of here as quickly as possible.

That is, if she'll start. I hadn't considered that when I decided to flee Washington after getting the ring back. Instead, I went to an outdoor clothing store and bought snowboard pants and other assorted winter wear to protect me from high-speed frostbite. While charging the clothes on credit cards already laden with debt from my Down Under mission, I hadn't considered whether Lucille might not be up to the task.

*Please, please start! You do that for me and I'll make it up to you, I swear. I'll take you to the shop, the fancy one that overcharges, and have you fixed from the front tire to the taillights. Just get me the hell out of here!*

I throw my leg over her saddle, pull her upright and draw in the kickstand with my heel. Her tire pressure feels low, probably due to the cold. On the way over in the cab I saw a bank with a digital display saying it's about twenty-five degrees. The tires will be fine until I can get her to a gas station. Besides, low pressure is good in the snow. The streets around here are covered.

I shift my weight on Lucille. She's emitting a creaking noise someplace in the rear. I rock her back and forth to see if anything is going to fall off. So far . . . good enough. I take a deep breath and blow it out hard before inserting the key.

*This is it. Come on. I need this.*

The lights on the dash flicker. Then I close my eyes and press the ignition button. For a second, nothing. Lucille is quiet. My heart drops.

But then she emits a wheeze.

*Err, err, err!*

I try again.

*Errr, errr, errr errr!*

"Come on! I need to get out of here!" I plead aloud while rocking her back and forth some more, hoping the sloshing around of her vital fluids will be enough to awake her from a deep, sickly winter slumber.

"Come on! Come on!"

I panic at the prospect of not being able to get away from here. I need to get out, far from my ex and the pain she inflicted on me yesterday and every day these last five months.

*Errrr, errrr, errrr, errrr . . .*

*You can do it. I know you can.*

*Errrrrr, errrrr, errrrr, errrrr . . .* She was gasping and choking while trying to shake off all that inertia.

*Errrrrr, errrrrr, errrrrr, errrrrr . . . pada, pada, pada pada . . . vrooooooommmmm!*

Lucille catches the beat like a cardiac patient brought back from the dead with a jolt to the chest. I pull back the throttle. She wails like an angry German shepherd with strep throat, initially pissed to be awakened from her slumber, then thrilled to be unleashed. I give her a little time to warm up and she settles into a reasonable rhythm. I ease her off the back patio, steer carefully in first gear across the snow-covered yard, my backpack resting on the saddle to keep the weight off my shoulders, and bump down off the curb onto the icy street.

I'm so goddamn delighted that Lucille started that I have no idea where I'm going. Wisps of snow blow across recently plowed streets of the suburban sprawl just outside DC. The biting cold and deep winter darkness makes it feel like 2 a.m., though it's only 6:30.

*OK, I need to head south.*

*Which way is that?*

I decided just this morning that I was going to return to Miami because I don't really have anyplace else to go. I emailed my friend Bruce—I used to rent a place from him—and asked him if I could come back.

"Sure," he replied right away. "Key's in the usual place if I'm not here. When are you coming?"

I don't tell him when or how I'm getting there. I'm not sure how long the trip will take in this weather and in my current condition of only having one good eye. I'm not entirely sure I can even do this. Riding on the highway without any real vision on my right side could very well be the last stupid decision I ever make.

But I don't care. I just need to get the fuck away from here. From her.

*How do I get south?*

*I need that road that got me here—what is it again?*

I'm still having problems with my memory. The doctors checked my head when I got hit, no word of permanent damage. But something is off. Without a baseline comparison of my brain before I was shot, it's hard for them to tell whether I was adversely affected. I know I can't remember the fucking highway I took all the way here. I used to ride it almost every day in Miami.

*That's where it ends. You take it all the way to Key Biscayne, it goes into US-1. That, I remember.*

*Fuck! This is torture!*

Maybe it's the cold freezing the neurons in my brain. I refuse to look up the road. I've got to recall this without the help of the Internet. Gotta get my mind right. But I can't remember other stuff. I recently spent half a day torturing myself to come up with the name of the actor who was Mel Gibson's partner in all the *Lethal Weapon* movies, repeating under my breath his catchphrase "Riggs!" mimicking his raspy voice till I blurted out his name while in line at Whole Foods.

"Damnit! Danny Glover!"

I'm going to figure this out, too. Arlington is on Lee Highway. I'll turn down there toward DC.

*There's a road off of Lee that I need to catch. Washington Parkway. Right. Does that go north or south? I think north, but I can go south from there. There's a south sign on there somewhere.*

Once on the parkway, I ratchet up my speed and feel the wind blasting its arctic chill against the thin sliver of exposed skin on my neck.

*Ugh, this is painful. And stupid. But fun. I need this.*

The parkway leads into Route 495, north and south. I take the southern spur and open the throttle to 70 miles per hour. With the wind chill it must be minus a billion degrees. Despite wearing two pairs of gloves and having my heated handgrips on high, my fingers feel permafrosted to the handlebars after 20 minutes.

*Let's see, let's see, let's see. It's here, I know it is.*

*Where's that road?*

Fog in my helmet's visor builds up when I slow down in traffic, forcing me to lift it to see the signs. My reduced speed also gives me a much-needed reprieve from the chill numbing my fingers and toes, though now the tip of my nose is burning from the frost.

*Where are you, road? I know I'm going to find you someplace.*

I'm kicking myself at my pride and refusal to google the highway, spiraling headlong into self-loathing and renewed fears that I've suffered permanent brain damage. Then, there it is, illuminated for all the world to see, but seemingly just for me, jarring my brain back from the brink of self-induced insanity.

**I-95 South, Richmond.**

*Thank you, once-forgotten highway! Now get me the fuck out of here!*


The bitter cold keeps me from making serious miles. After an hour of riding, I'm still barely outside of DC, somewhere in the middle of bumfuck Virginia. This riding-at-night business isn't going to work. Not at this time of year. If I'm going to make a cannonball run to sun-soaked Southern Florida in the dead of winter with one mirror, one good eye, and a bike in desperate need of a tune-up, I'm going to have to be smart about it. I'll only ride during the daylight hours when it's slightly warmer. That's the responsible thing to do, I reason. I congratulate myself on my maturity.

I find a Motel 6, pull in, plunk down another credit card with a little more wiggle room on it and get a room on the first floor so I can keep an eye on Lucille. Desk clerks at joints like these know riders want their bikes close. Some riders would probably pull their bikes inside if they could get them through the door. I ride Lucille around to the back of the building and find my room.

*You did good today, girl. I'm proud of you.*

I give her a little love tap on the tank, then head indoors to thaw. The room has a stale odor of the BO of 10,000 previous occupants, but I don't care. I strip off my frosted winter garb, slip out of the rest of my clothes, and take an hour-long scalding shower, hoping I won't lose any of my still-numb digits to frostbite.


"So why are you doing this again?" Tatiana asks over the phone me as I'm about to take off amid a frozen drizzle the following morning. I make up some half-assed reason for returning to Miami, saying I need to pack up my place down there.

"It just seems really stupid to ride in the middle of winter, when you can't see very well." She's making a good point, though I am loath to admit it to her and especially myself.

"It's fine. I'm fine. I can see," I assure her while adjusting my backpack straps and getting ready to take off.

"No, you can't! Even Dan thinks you're being stupid!" she says, referring to our mutual friend who photographed me in the hospital and has a reckless streak a mile wide.

Tatiana's protests enrage me. I tell her to leave me alone and hang up. I don't want her concern. The very concept of concern is repellent.

*I do whatever I want. I earned it. Sorry if you don't like it, Tatiana.*

Same goes for everyone else. I exist for me. I'm only alive by freak chance. I should be dead. Every moment since I was shot is stolen. As such, how I choose to spend those moments is my own self-involved, inconsiderate business.

I put on my helmet and race out of the parking lot amid a steady rain that makes it nearly impossible to see.


Over the next two days, Virginia's countryside turns into the backwoods of the Carolinas. A persistent rain follows me. Most of the time I ride through it. When it pours hard, I can barely make out what's in front of me or monitor my speed. Several times, tractor-trailers snuck up on my blind side, spraying me with wash from their eighteen wheels and making me swerve toward the median.

Near the Georgia border, the weather finally breaks and the air warms up. I stop for gas and shed some layers. I check my phone and see an email from my ex:

**xxxxxxxxx@hotmail.com:**
**I was just thinking back to when you effeminately sat in Ceci's office and told her you were "afraid" of me. Oh my God! Do you realize how every male (and female) friend I have thinks you are a HUGE PUSSY? Way back then everyone thought I should dump your effeminate ass and**

**I almost dug your ugly ring from the bottom of my purse to hand the box back to you. I had it in me to try and try even though I was done with you emotionally. How was I ever going to be attracted to such a prick again? How do you honestly take yourself seriously? My only fault was feeling bad and not wanting to totally break it off with you because you were trying so hard to keep me. Ugh. My lesson learned was I should have ended that nonsense right there. Maybe you should just come out of the closet. You are either gay or a total, complete puss.**

She's referring to our failed therapy sessions with a relationship counselor named Ceci last spring. That was before I went to Afghanistan and got hurt. What a waste that was.

Nothing in her message is new ground. Couple things confounded me, though. What's with "puss"? Why wouldn't she just call me a "pussy"? Is "puss" a greater insult than "pussy"? Is her hatred so great it causes her to miss keystrokes? And "gay"? Really? Who uses "gay" as an insult anymore?

She is right about one thing: I was afraid of her and told the counselor both in private and during couples sessions. I thought my fear was justified. She's a federal agent with an explosive temper, a firearm, and a tendency to overimbibe. I'm certain in drunken moments she's thought about killing me. She'd probably get away with it too. Fake a struggle after she popped me in the temple, then put a bullet in the wall, maybe even clip herself in the fleshy part of the upper arm to make it look like I tried killing her.

I might be a "puss," but justifiably so.

I stop in Tampa to do something that will not only lighten my physical load, albeit ever-so-slightly, but hopefully rid me of the emotional anvil hanging around my neck: I'm going to sell this goddamn engagement ring.

Tatiana is from Tampa and recommended a couple places that would give me a good price.

However, a "good price" in the used engagement ring game is apparently only a fraction of what you pay for your everlasting token of commitment. The first jeweler I went to offered me a thousand bucks. That weasel eyeballed the stone and talked down the resale value, saying the cut I chose is not this year's favorite. And according to his well-rehearsed shtick, used engagement rings are like herpes: the taint never goes away. "It's the best offer you're going to get," he says dismissively while placing the ring back in the box.

I grab the ring and storm out.

"Fucking piece of shit."

In the parking lot, I stare at the box, the contents of which cost me more than I make during two months in Afghanistan, and take deep, frenzied breaths.

*Calm down.*

*There's another place she recommended.*

*It's not far from here.*

*Try your luck there.*

Outside the next jewelry store I take a moment to plan my sale's strategy:

*Don't let him see your desperation to get rid of this thing. Eyes up and bright.*

*Don't mention the words "engagement" or "broken." In fact, say as little as possible.*

*Don't plead. He'll sense your desperation like a jungle predator smells fear.*

Having talked myself up, I head into the store and offer my wares to the man behind the counter. He eyes the ring through his jeweler's lens for a few moments, twisting it to take in its angles and shape. Then he turns his scrutinizing eye toward me.

"Do you have the paperwork?

I produce the certificate authenticating the carat and quality and to make sure I didn't steal the thing. Whether I'm a failure at romance is of no consequence. All that matters to these diamond fiends feigning a moral compass is that I'm not a thief who's going to bring the cops down on him.

"I can give you $1,500 for it," he says, placing it on the counter between us.

I stand there motionless, stone silent. That's still less than a third of what I paid for it. I'm getting hosed on this deal. I want to pick the thing up and slice the side of his face with the edge of platinum mounting that cradles that stupid fucking diamond.

I look at it laying there between us, remembering how happy I was when I bought it.

*You're an idiot, you know that?*

I remember slipping it on her finger and the pleasure we took in keeping it our little secret for a couple of weeks until we could tell her parents and mine.

*What was I thinking?*

It seems so embarrassing now. I'm horrified by my naiveté—even more so than her deception and cruelty. I just want to forget the whole thing.

*Never again!*

"I'll take it," I tell the jeweler.

He counts out fifteen one hundred dollar bills that I slip in my wallet, then bolt out the door.


Over the bridge that divides Tampa from its southern sister city, St. Petersburg, I pull back the throttle to hasten my escape. Lucille screams and shakes violently when I rip past 90 miles an hour on my way to a criminally irresponsible one hundred. I can barely make out the shapes of cars rapidly shrinking in the reflection of my single, vibrating side-view mirror. She can't go much faster than that.

Right now, she can't go fast enough. I need to put as many miles between that ring and me as quickly as possible.

When the city fades from sight, I bring her down to a reasonable 75 miles per hour so I can at least try to enjoy the view. The pristine waters of the Gulf of Mexico sparkle on my right in the early afternoon sun. I'm about an hour away from my parents' condo in Venice, the sleepiest town in all of Florida. They're down there with my sister, her husband, and my nephews. I said I'd stop by on my way to Miami.

When I roll up to their condo, the boys are outside checking out a lizard, mesmerized by its green hue.

"Hey Uncle Carmen," says Thomas, a greeting style he picked up from his mother. Frankie says nothing. He looks at me for a moment, then resumes his examination of the local wildlife.

I head for the door, on the other side of which is a cacophony of voices so loud one would expect to find dozens of drunken sailors on shore leave crammed in their two-bedroom condo.

My family yells a lot. Not in anger. That's just how they talk. That one table in a restaurant wrecking the ambiance with their high-decibel chatter, that's them. The loudest among the adults is also the most diminutive. My sister is all of five-foot-two but can outshout anyone. I can hear every word she says while standing outside.

"She acts like she knows eeeeeveeeryything!" Tara's saying about someone I don't know, which isn't uncommon considering how little effort we make to stay in touch. I know next to nothing about her other than she's worked in banking for twenty years. I know even less about her husband.

It's always been like this with my family and me, though the degree of civility varies. My mother and I can't spend five minutes together without one or both of us misconstruing something the other said and taking offense. As a young child, through my tyrannical teenage years and into adulthood, we never got along. When I lived in Egypt, then Brazil, I'd come home a couple weeks a year, usually for Christmas. By the end of those visits, she and I were barely speaking, both hoping to avoid another blow up. Lately, it's only gotten worse. Since that day in the emergency room, when I wished aloud that I'd been killed in Afghanistan, we've barely spoken at all.

My father and I can, and do, talk, though our conversations almost never delve into personal matters. I was genuinely shocked a few years ago when he once asked me, "How's your love life?"

As for my nephews, I do make some effort to engage them the few hours a year I spend with them. But they are largely foreign to me, as I surely am to them. I tell myself I want to know them better, but do little to make it happen.

I'm largely responsible for this chasm between my family and me because I keep them at arm's length. I divulge little about myself to them and as such have no intention of telling them what I've been through these last few days and how just a few hours ago I sold the engagement ring I gave to my ex for the modest wad of cash in my back pocket.

I enter the living room midstream of their conversation hoping to go unnoticed.


After dinner, Thomas is teasing his brother relentlessly, trying to goad him into unleashing the anger for which Frankie is famous.

Not failing to disappoint, Frankie goes Category Five ballistic and amidst his tantrum throws all of our shoes in the garbage, then hides under a table to cry. My parents and sister laugh. "He'll grow out of it," my mother says.

I'm tempted to tell them that I know from experience how hurtful their teasing can be. I was the same way as Frankie at his age: prone to bouts of screaming and terrible tantrums that roused my sister and parents to fits of laughter. Some of my most vivid memories are of them teasing me. It wasn't until I was older that I realized their ridicule wasn't intentionally malicious, rather a misguided expression of affection. Instead of hugs in our family, we poke fun till someone cries to show we care because none of us is particularly adept at genuine displays of emotion. I'm guilty of the same. I don't tease my nephews, but I've been told by many a girlfriend I teased them too much and told them I cared too little.

I still carry around that childhood resentment of my own teasing even though as a grown man I know damn well I should get over it. But I can't. Forgiveness doesn't come easily to me or other members of my family. It's one of our worst traits.

I want to warn Frankie about indulging that anger, tell him to not let it control his life and make decisions rooted in fury. I want to tell him how I've already made those mistakes, let my ego and anger be a guiding force in my life, how for too long I doused my anger with intoxicants that made it much worse. Even though I quit alcohol and hard drugs years ago, I want to tell him that my recklessness and anger persists. I fight it every day. Most of the time I lose.

I want to tell him so he can avoid making the same mistakes. If he's smart, he'll recognizes his tendencies early and deal with them better as an adult.

But not now. A five-year-old isn't ready to hear that, especially one that is panting and crying under the dining room table while his parents and grandparents are doubled over laughing.

The next morning, I take off from my parents' condo and ride down the coast, then head east along Route 41, otherwise known as Alligator Alley, the highway connecting the west coast of Southern Florida to Miami. On the straightaway I gun Lucille up to 95 miles per hour, then ease off the throttle to enjoy the warm, humid air and rain-slicked highway. Water beads on my bare forearms.

By afternoon, I pull into Bruce's driveway in Coral Gables, a small, upscale town adjacent to Miami. He's not home, so I use the secret key to open the door to my previous and now current home: a tiny garage-turned-one-bed-room bungalow, replete with kitchenette and sixties-era couch upholstered in pumpkin orange and turd-brown polyester fabric.

Not long ago I was sharing this place with my ex. I wasn't sure how I'd feel about returning to the scene of our relationship's demise. Now I know, and I'm already regretting it.

Not all of it was bad. We did have a few good moments here before everything fell apart.

When my ex and I returned from Pittsburgh a newly minted engaged couple, we immediately began planning our wedding, choosing a venue and discussing our catering options. We even considered marrying in secret right away and then having a formal ceremony later on. That's how giddy we were.

Our bliss however was soon interrupted by seismic rumbling in Haiti. We'd been engaged for less than two weeks when the earthquake struck claiming thousands of lives and destroying large parts of the country's capital.

I went down to Haiti to cover the devastation and relief effort. Meanwhile, she was tasked with helping bolster security at the US embassy in Port-au-Price. We spent weeks apart doing our respective jobs, though in close proximity, only seeing each one once on the street and just for a few moments. The situation in Haiti grim: bodies were picked up, loaded into dump trucks and hauled to mass graves. Everywhere you looked there was sorrow and wreckage. Everyone had lost at least one person they loved. I'd warned my ex before embarking that the situation there would be life altering for her.

"You're going to see things there you can't unsee," I remember telling her, in our tiny shared home, before we left for Haiti. She assured me she could handle it. And I believed she could.

A month after the quake we were both back in Miami, thrilled to be reunited. But something had changed. My ex was sullen, drew inward, and drank heavily. At first I said nothing, feeling like a hypocrite considering my own past problems with alcohol. Then I tried talking to her, which didn't go over well. She began frequently listing all the things she disliked about me. My lackluster housekeeping efforts and the ants in our bedroom were the fodder for hours-long arguments over our fundamental differences including my atheism and her growing contempt for journalists of all stripes—particularly me, apparently. She spent less time here and more at her parents' house, or so I thought. Going over the timeline of our relationship now, I think that's when she started seeing that other guy. I can't be sure.

I do know that the less time we were together, the more tenuous our connection became. I fell into old habits and looked for something far way to distract me from problems at home. When the opportunity to go to Iraq for two months came up, I grabbed it thinking the distance might do us some good. Although when I returned she was more distant and angry at me than ever. Confused and hurt, I left again—that time for Afghanistan. Our relationship in tatters, we maintained the facade of still being engaged and agreed to work on our relationship. However, we soon discovered that couples separated by 7,000 nautical miles aren't ideally positioned for working out the more serious kinks in a relationship. Instead, we traded snipes back and forth via email. Then she stopped responding. I, in turn, decided to join the soldiers at PK on a patrol through a remote village on the last day of Ramadan.

# CHAPTER 22
# GRAHAM GREENE CAN SUCK MY DICK!

JANUARY, 30, 2011
CORAL GABLES, FLORIDA

The "Failure Cave," what I've come to call my abode behind Bruce's house, is just the way I left it last summer. My books and clothes, a motorcycle helmet in the closet, a dinged-up surfboard under the bed, all where I left them. A few of her things are still here too. A pair of socks, a book I bought for her.

Nothing's changed, except for me. This isn't my place anymore. These are my things, but I don't belong here. I'm certainly not the same person I was. Being here makes that all the more obvious. That life is long gone.

While going through the artifacts of my former self, I thumb through the pages of one of my books, Graham Greene's *The Comedians*. It's a story of betrayal, false pretenses, and adultery set against the backdrop of Haiti's Papa Doc regime. I skim its pages before settling on one of the underlined passages. The novel's protagonist, Brown, receives a letter from his married lover, Martha, while he's in New York searching for someone to buy his Port-au-Prince hotel.

She writes to him about how the "sexual life" is the greatest test one can endure and that the key to happiness in love is to do so with "charity to those we love and with affection to those we have betrayed." This I remember.

If the sexual life is the greatest test, then I need to go back to preschool and start all over. I couldn't have screwed up my own love life any more than I have in the last few weeks.

Tatiana recently discovered while snooping through my email that I went Down Under with Fernanda. The two have been commiserating about my deception ever since. They even cc'd me on a few of their messages while trying to parse just how I managed to dupe them. Both are furious. There's no explaining my way out of the horrendous mess I've created, no reasoning that justifies my behavior. I can't even claim residual emotional trauma from my injury. Neither of them would buy that bullshit considering how calculating I was in my deception, which they take great pains to remind me.

Not that it's any consolation to them, but I do feel unspeakably shitty, though that raises the question whether I'd feel the same had I gotten away with it. I'd like to think I would, but seeing that I didn't feel bad until I was caught answers that question for me. I thought about offering some kind of apology to Tatiana, telling her that I've been "faithful" since returning from that trip. However, bragging about my recent fidelity is vaguely akin to a serial killer boasting he hasn't gone on a homicidal spree in weeks. As for Fernanda, I already decided to leave the subject alone and never respond to her email telling me what a jerk I am. This is the second time I've hurt her—there's no apology I can offer that will be even remotely helpful.


The ceiling fan whirls violently in the darkness. I inadvertently rolled over on its remote control in the middle of the night and cranked up the blade speed to about 8,000 RPM. I like that I don't have to get out of bed to dim the lights or adjust the fan. I can just lie here as long as I like, though my bladder is telling me it's about to explode. These last few weeks I've had very little reason to get out of bed other than the call of nature and the occasional pizza delivery, and even less motivation to do anything other than wallow in self-pity and try to sleep off my guilt. I can actually feel Tatiana's disdain like it's a concentrated beam of hatred fired from her apartment in Brooklyn, traveling a thousand-plus miles and permeating the roof of The Failure Cave. Same from Fernanda in Rio. Yet a third from my ex, wherever the hell she is, creating a Death-Star–like triangulation of pure scorn focused on me and burrowing a hole in my forehead. Four months after getting shot with an RPG and I've squandered all the good will and sympathy sex a person could accrue in my situation.

Right now, I'd give anything to duck away, shut my eyes, click my heels and be back in Afghanistan. A stroll through a rural village teeming with the Taliban would be a delight at this point. I wouldn't mind even getting hurt again. Not in the face this time. And certainly no lost limbs. Maybe just a bullet to the fleshy part of the thigh, hell even a buttock. It'd be apt punishment for the shit I pulled. Maybe then I wouldn't feel so terrible all the time.

# CHAPTER 23
# FINAL TOUCHES ON A FLAWED MASTERPIECE

MARCH 1, 2011
NEW YORK CITY

There's a new addition to the Super Friends Team of Surgeons tasked with putting me back together. I drag myself out of the Failure Cave and back to New York to meet with Dr. Auran.

A few days before the operation, he walks me through the procedure. It seems fairly simple. First I'll be lightly sedated, perhaps even in a twilight state where I'm cognizant of what's happening. Then he'll stitch in place the lens that will make it possible for me to see out of my right eye for the first time in six months. He tells me my vision won't be perfect. But I will be able to make out shapes and get the general gist of the world, which is much better than the amorphous blobs of light I currently see. As he's explaining this to me, I can tell he's looking for a certain excitement in my face at the prospect of being almost whole again. I feign the enthusiasm he expects, but just can't seem to muster the thrill I should be feeling. I can't help but realize that I'm undergoing another surgery all alone. The whole "stick a needle in my eye" idea doesn't exactly have me jazzed, either.

The next day I take an early-morning taxi back to the hospital, head up to ophthalmology, check in, strip, put on my ass-breezy gown, and lie on the gurney to await the procedure. I'm an old hand at this routine by now. A nurse pinches me with an IV. I wince and curse quietly. I'll never get used to that. The meds start to kick in. "Count backwards from twenty." By seventeen, the tears well up.

Alone and under the knife again.


Awake.

Blink.

*Where am . . .*

*Wait . . .*

*I've got it.*

Compared to my first three surgeries, I feel fairly coherent. The meds they gave me this time were much lighter and I'm told the operation lasted less than an hour. I've only been out for a few. I look up at the ceiling, then down toward the door. I see it. I see it with both eyes. There it is. But something is . . . off. The door jamb, it's . . . I don't know . . . wavy. The line of the frame doesn't run straight down. When I look with my newly repaired right eye while covering the other it's off-kilter, like a funhouse passageway. I test my repaired eye on other objects. The railing of the bed is wrinkled. My fingers held out as far as I can appear bent, each digit has a fuzzy halo. Dr. Auran comes in and asks me how I feel. I tell him I can see, but not as well as I thought I might.

"Give it time," he says. "As it heals, your vision will improve."

The doctors told me my vision will never be perfect, that the wrinkle in my retina will always make objects seem out of sorts. Reading with my right eye is not an option. Glasses may improve some of my sight but will never restore it to normal. I'll just have to adjust. I know all of this—I was told months ago while recuperating in the Washington Heights apartment. But I never fully accepted that my eyesight will be forever damaged as long as I had another surgery to undergo. Still incomplete, I could fantasize about seeing the world again through two good eyes, have my full depth perception back. I dreamed I'd stop bumping into furniture due to my blind spots and ramming my right shoulder into doorways after miscalculating my entry.

Now that dream is over and I'm forced to face the reality that I'll never be like I was. I wasn't ready for this. Vainly, I start trying to find my own fixes.

*Maybe I can just keep the bad one shut all the time. If I do, will the skin around that eye be wrinklier, like a photographer's? Maybe I really should wear a patch like I'd schemed all those months ago when I thought I was going to lose my eye. No, it's too dramatic. I can't walk around with that thing all the time. I don't want people staring at me. I got a taste of what that feels like when I had the shield taped to my face. No thanks.*

I lie back and weigh my fashion options for the future and a potential long life viewed between two distinct fields of vision.

*I'll get used to it. Sure. It won't be all that bad.*

As I'm telling myself this, I'm already getting a headache right behind my eyes from using both at the same time. My new dual, yet uneven vision is causing my head to pound while a relentless itch infests my right eye. It feels like Auran inserted a rusty pie plate between the lid and eyeball.

*What the hell?*

The nurse tells me it's going to itch for a while and to avoid the temptation to rub or touch my eye unless I want the new stitch in my eyeball to get infected and blind me permanently.

"Not really," I say, trying to sound nonchalant about her warning. But the itch is so irritating I contemplate the cost/benefit ratio of not rubbing it and saving my eye versus the discomfort I'm currently experiencing.

*Fuck me, fuck me, fuck me. This is the worst.*

The nurse administers a dose of cooling eye drops and the itching eases for a few minutes before it starts itching again. She tells me it's going to be that way for a few days.

In the meantime, I'm instructed to rest. But not in the hospital. I'm being discharged. Right now, in fact. In at 8:00 in the morning and out by 1:00 in the afternoon. No lollygagging. Me and my newly repaired eyeball are back on the street, taking on the lightning-fast pace of Manhattan a mere five hours after my arrival.

I get on the subway without incident, checking out the assortment of passengers with my new artificial lens. I shut my left eye to check everyone out. Faces are still blurry, but features recognizable.

*So I won't be able to see all that well. I still have one good eye. I'll get by. I have no choice.*

I stare at my hands again and the halos around my fingers giving them a mystical aura reminiscent of my acid-dropping days, when everything had that glow of resplendent potential and wonder. But that was a lifetime ago, before I learned about the stark reality of places like, say, Afghanistan, where there's less opportunity for fanciful dreaming amid the backdrop of decades of war. Then again, a lot of folks there do use opium and heroin. It's not the same, though. Opiates are an analgesic for the intolerable cruelty of life amid never-ending war.

*Acid is about enlightenment.*

*I smoked lots of opium when I was younger. That time with my college girl-friend Delilah. We inhaled a sweet, fragrant bowl, then had our first kiss.*

*The opium we smoked was just like in Afghanistan . . .*

*I went to Afghanistan . . .*

*Again and again and again . . .*

"Columbus Circle, with transfers to the . . . "

*What? Whoa . . . This is your stop.*

I'd fallen into a semilucid sleep. Whatever they knocked me out with clearly hasn't worn off.

I get off the train, then head for the stairs that will take me to the southwest corner of Central Park. Outside it's a drizzly, miserable day. The wind is biting. I shrug my shoulders and lean into it. I'm supposed to keep my eye covered in blustery conditions, really all conditions, especially since I just walked out of the hospital less than an hour ago. Should have taken a taxi, but I don't care. I feel nothing but the wind. Even the itch in my eye is gone. I'm taking my rebuilt baby blue out for a test drive.

My hotel is just a few blocks away. I cross over 58th Street and head down 8th Avenue. The world appears in another dimension that I'd forgotten existed over the last six months. I need to acclimate. Curb distances are re-calibrated on the fly.

*Careful. Watch your feet. There you go. Step up.*

*Not so high that you look like you're straddling a fence, you weirdo.*

*Try to be less dramatic on the next block.*

I wait for the light to change with the other pedestrians bunched up on the corner. In Midtown there always seems to be a critical mass of commuters piling into one another, about to push those at the front into oncoming traffic just before the light changes. This time I bound off the curb less clumsily, dare I say suavely, and summit onto the opposite sidewalk with ease.

Now for the ultimate test: I'm going to scurry across four lanes of break-neck traffic to the Milford Plaza Hotel without getting killed. I amp up the danger level a little more by jaywalking between the two intersections.

*New eye, don't fail me now.*

I scan the street for cars coming up the one-way thoroughfare, check for errant bike messengers—against the grain or with the flow—then scramble like hell for the hotel. Dash, stutter, step, let a cab whiz by, then haul ass for the other side. No problem at all. I've got my renewed, though certainly not improved, biocular view of the world down pat.


I like the Milford Plaza Hotel, despite it being several decades beyond its prime. It's a remnant of Old New York, a once swanky hot spot just off Broadway that now caters to budget-minded travelers from the Midwest and the occasional Brazilian tourists, which seems to be more and more frequent these days. I've been hearing a lot of Portuguese in the city and signs in some of the stores tell would-be customers A GENTE FALA PORTUGUES (We speak Portuguese). They've got dough because their currency is strong and their economy is thriving, while the rest of the world remains, well, maybe not in the shitter, but certainly clinging to the underside of the bowl while trying to climb out.

Before our falling out in Brooklyn and my yellow-bellied retreat, Tatiana joined me here on a few occasions when I came to town to see my doctors. I was expensing it to CBS, so why not have her over for a few rounds of always-erotic hotel sex? Once, after coupling on the Milford Plaza single-digit thread count sheets (at least I hope being cheap is the reason I'm itchy and not the bedbug epidemic plaguing the city), we joked about how if we ever spawned a daughter due to our negligence we'd name her "Millie" after the hotel where she was likely conceived. This kind of loose talk about accidental procreation always got us riled up again. Of course, Tatiana would go gaga over this talk, telling me she'd be pleased as punch to have my baby, hoping that our recklessness in the sack would make the decision to become parents a moot point.

How I never knocked her up seems inconceivable as I lie on my Milford Plaza bed alone, ruminating on our erotic adventures here.

*Best not to go there. Leave her alone. You hurt her too much. She's better off without you.*

I keep telling myself this while opening my laptop. I want to check out how my eye works staring at it. After a few minutes I'm already getting a headache. But if I close the bad eye, it's OK.

*Where's my eye patch?*

I dig it out of my bag.

*That's better. Much, much better. This will just have to do from now on. Adjust and move on.*

Just then an email from Tatiana pops up. She knows I'm in town for my surgery. Maybe she's ready to bury the hatchet. Maybe she wants to see how the procedure went. Maybe she wants to come over and comfort me like she did after my first surgeries way back in September. Maybe I'm gonna get lucky tonight.

*Wait, no.*

*Don't do that.*

*You can't lead her on.*

*Leave her alone!*

I begin weighing my options: maintain some semblance of moral integrity or head back down the dark path.

*If she asks to come over, I'll say no.*

*Wait, no. I'll tell her she can come over, but nothing can happen between us . . .*

*OK, if she does comes over, and tries any funny business, I'll flat-out resist.*

*No. Here it is. I'll give in only if she's really insistent and absolutely agrees it's just physical.*

*Yes. That's it. Foolproof.*

I click on her email.

**xxxxxxxx@gmail.com**
**if i were you, id stick to banging stewardesses and dog walkers. you can't handle women with brains . . .**

Despite Tatiana's assertion, I hadn't been bedding dog walkers and stewardesses, just a Brazilian lawyer and her, both of whom are exceptionally bright.

While I do take full responsibly for my abhorrent behavior of late, a tiny part of me thinks I deserve some contextual, and even ancestral, leeway on this one.

Yeah, I shouldn't have rendezvoused with Fernanda in Australia behind Tatiana's back. That was a dick move bordering on evil. But in my physical and emotional state, I thought I deserved an additional dalliance and figured Tatiana would never find out.

And in my search for other flimsy excuses I fall back on the one that's my go-to when I've done something truly horrible: I've got some serious wickedness in my family tree.

One of my dad's most memorable stories from his childhood is about my great-grandmother Rose, who was blind. One day, when he was about eight years old, Rose called my dad into the laundry room where she was filling the basin with water.

"Give me one of those kittens," she said, referring to the litter born at their house a week earlier. My dad recalls dutifully handing her a kitten, which she took by the scruff and held under water until it was drowned.

"Give me another one." She repeated the process until the entire litter was dead.

Whenever I catch myself doing something particularly cruel or inconsiderate, I tell myself to stop "drowning the kittens." However by that time it's usually too late. And right now there are a whole lot of dead kittens in the tub.

# CHAPTER 24
# INSTANT REPLAY

APRIL 8, 2011
NORTH MIAMI, FLORIDA

I'm not even sure it works. It's been in storage for more than six months. That whole time I haven't even tried to turn it on. The battery must be dead.

*Where's the charger?*

I dig through my gear bag and come up with the right one. I try pulling the battery out of my video camera. It's stuck. The spring-loaded release is broken. Probably the rest of the camera, too. I haven't so much as run a damp rag over the filthy thing since I got it back after being shot. There are dried, crusty droplets of my blood on the lens hood and handle. The body is caked in mud and grit. I dropped it in the dirt when the rocket hit me in the side of the head. It laid on the floor of the armored truck when I was evacuated, then my lap, accounting for the blood and phlegm from when I was dry heaving.

*There's no way this thing still works.*

I haven't been able to muster the courage to turn it on, to see if I captured the attack on video. After more than six months of wondering, though, I'm compelled by my own morbid curiosity to see if I caught it despite the crippling fear that seeing the attack will destroy what's left of my fractured psyche.

It's time I find out one way or another. This back-and-forth has torn at me ever since I opened the box delivered to my apartment that contained all my gear from PK. I need to face the terror.

I head over to the house of my friend Brian, the Voice of America Latin America correspondent in whose office I used to loaf. He's a whiz-bang video editor and my go-to guru for all things camera related. I am woefully ignorant about the inner workings and advanced settings of my own gear. I'm a print guy with cameras, not a videographer. If it's compelling, I'll capture it. It'll be in focus, but certainly not winning any awards.

Brian rolls his eyes when I pull the camera out of the bag and tell him I have yet to fire it up. I want him to do it for me. He puts in the battery, noting the horrific condition of my most expensive piece of gear, and flips it on. Surprising both of us, the camera comes to life, emitting a low hum reminiscent of the sound made by the proton packs in *Ghostbusters*.

"Let's see if you got it," Brian says while hooking up the camera to his laptop.

The "it" in question is the rocket attack. I'd been filming during that entire afternoon up to the moment I was hit: the pre-mission brief, the dirt road through the tiny village lined with stone and mud houses, wild marijuana growing everywhere. I remember talking to the two young men on the side of the road. That hinky vibe. Something's wrong. Then, that sound. The rocket racing toward me. I remember feeling like all the oxygen was being sucked out of my chest. I turned, watching it beeline. I've relived that moment a million times, watched it play out right up to the moment of impact. It is my clearest, most comprehensive memory.

Here at Brian's home office, it's all come to life, the guys walking up a narrow path along a small hillside above the village's dirt road. Zotto and Wyckoff are in frame when we hear explosions in the distance, another fight a few valleys away. There we are snickering while walking among the waist-high pot plants. Then head back to the road. An old man washes his hands in a stream. He's preparing for the end-of-Ramadan feast. We shouldn't be here. This is a holy time. A time of celebration and joy. This is wrong. Too quiet.

Brian is watching the video. "Is this it?" he asks.

It is. This is it.

"It should be coming up," I say, trying to strike an outward air of composure while I'm terrorized by my worst moment and nightmare about to play out in front of me. I feel like I'm about to witness my own execution. "Right as I'm talking to these guys," I point to the screen. Brian leans in. I pull back. In a flash their faces slacken as they look toward the sound of the *WHOOSH!* That sound was already permanently seared onto the part of my brain where recurring horrors are stored. The rocket impacts my face a fraction later, a dull thud as it strikes my cheek. I see it again. Not on camera. I didn't catch the rocket hitting my head. But I can see it as clearly as if it were playing on the screen in front of me. Seeing the video has unbottled some dormant details. The long trace of the rocket's path. It seemed to arc and correct course midflight, as if it were programmed to hit only me, targeted for a deadly headshot. I watch it knowing I'll soon be gone. There's no escape even though time slowed down, allowing me a last thought before I am nothing.

*WHAM!*

The image shakes violently before settling hard on the ground. The camera is still recording, its lens focused on the dirt path.

For a moment, the village and Brian's office are still.

In the village, that voice asks: "Are you OK?"

"No, I'm not." I reply.

I'm not OK. Not then. And certainly not now. When the rocket hits, I jerk back in the chair and contort my whole body against a blow only I can see. The anguish is audible, but off camera. It is haunting in the absence of the visual, a moan from beyond the grave. I reach for my face, feel the scar tracing from the corner of my eye to the top of my cheek. I run my index finger over the titanium plate just below my eye socket, a tic I've developed when I think about the attack. It sticks out, creating a subtle asymmetry in my face. Pressing it slightly hurts immensely. I catch myself doing this when I feel bad about something, a Pavlovian punishment of my own twisted design.

*I really wish I hadn't just seen that.*

Pins and needles race up my spine, followed by flop sweat. I feel sick. I jump out of my chair, turn away from the screen as Brian's wife Jen puts a hand on my back.

"You OK?"

"Yeah, it's fine."

*Deep breath. Exhale. Nope. That's not gonna do it. I'm not OK. Far from OK. Nothing is OK. I may never be OK again.*

My back is to the monitor. The video is still running. I can hear myself ask: "Do I still have my eye?" Brian mercifully turns it off.

I harbor an irrational fear that my eye did pop out. Perhaps that's why I compulsively trace my fingers around my eye socket. It doesn't make sense, but it's there. That and other memories of the attack tinge everything else in my life. When I'm thirsty, I think of the hot wash of the helicopter's blades burning my throat when I was evacuated. That moment right before falling to sleep, the tranquil haze of twilight consciousness, reminds me of my weeks-long narcotic fog. Every thought, every moment, everything about me is tainted by that stupid fucking rocket attack. All else is a blurry afterthought. Losing my virginity, first love, the best wave I ever surfed—mere preamble leading up to the moment of impact. As it raced toward me, I accepted death as an inevitability. Now, the memory of my resignation to dying has left an indelible black mark on me that permeates every moment since.

"I need to talk to some cigarettes about this," I tell Brian and Jen before beating a hasty retreat from their home.

I tell them I'll be right back, which is a lie. I head out the door, get on my motorcycle and speed away from their house as quickly as I can. After putting enough distance between myself and that fucking video, I stop at a pharmacy. "Pack of Marlboro Reds and a lighter." Cowboy killers. Give the clerk a twenty. Don't bother to look at the change. Go outside, rip open the pack, put one between my lips and fire it up. The first drag sizzles like bacon grease. The greatest pleasures in life are always the worst for you.

I draw a dense thunderstorm-sized cloud of smoke into my lungs. Hold it, then blow out as if attempting to expel all my anger, fear, and resentment in one cathartic, carcinogenic fog.

*Still not gone. Let's try that again.*

*Nope. Still there.*

Inhale. Exhale. My breathing seems deeper than when I last smoked. It's been months. Some of the ill effects had surely subsided in the absence of cigarettes from my daily diet.

Persistent cough: gone.

Raspy voice: that's gone, too.

I talk aloud to see if my voice has changed after only half a cigarette.

"I hate myself for doing this."

# CHAPTER 25
# WHACKING THE BEARD

MAY 1, 2011
CORAL GABLES, FLORIDA

*Something's up.*

It's all over the place.

I need to find TV. The Failure Cave doesn't have one, but it's never occurred to me I was missing one until now. Not that I'm some lofty intellectual that doesn't pollute his mind with visual rubbish; I've just done little these last few months but fill my days with drivel on Netflix and recent theatrical releases pirated from bootleg websites.

*Wait, Bruce has a TV.*

But he's out of town covering the Royal Wedding. He's been away for work a lot lately, leaving me to stew alone. It's been weeks since I've held a prolonged conversation with someone. I've all but written off everyone else I know in Miami. I don't want to see them. They'll ask me questions like, "How are you doing?" that I can't answer unless they're expecting—and can handle—a really grim answer.

*Enough of your bitching.*

I key into Bruce's house and fumble with three different remotes for a television with a higher IQ than my own before finding one of the networks. Doesn't matter which one. They're all carrying the same event: The president's going to address the nation late tonight.

*It's gotta be huge.*

There's widespread speculation about what it could be. Rumors of a terror attack are flooding social media. Scrolling through my Twitter feed, I see Fox News is spit-balling that Libyan leader Muammar Qaddafi was killed.

Whatever it is, it's serious enough for POTUS to keep the nation guessing late into a Sunday night.

As the scheduled moment approaches, the White House tells Americans to wait a little longer. The president's address has been pushed back a half hour, ratcheting up the county's collective tension. Even I can feel it, and I've been largely disconnected from the world these last few months.

I'm also starting to get that old feeling, the rush of adrenaline and anxiety I get about a big story. I haven't felt much of anything lately other than fear, shame, and self-pity since the start of my South Florida exile.

The cable news commentators stop pontification midsentence as the president approaches the podium. Here we go.

"Good evening. Tonight, I can report to the American people and to the world that the United States has conducted an operation that killed Osama bin Laden, the leader of al Qaeda, and a terrorist who's responsible for the murder of thousands of innocent men, women, and children. It was nearly 10 years ago that a bright September day was darkened . . . "

*Holy shit!*

I pace around Bruce's living room gesticulating wildly and exclaiming inarticulate combinations of syllables as if I'd been raised by wolves and never learned a language. I try calming down to listen to the rest of his address—something about a compound in Pakistan and those that lost loved ones on Sept. 11.

Before he signs off, I've already started calculating what this might mean for me. These last few weeks I've been trying to get someone to send me back to Afghanistan. So far, no luck. But with bin Laden dead, surely Afghanistan will be a focal point for coverage.

Pangs of guilt hit me upon realizing what a self-centered prick I'm being about this.

*Not everything is about you, asshole.*

So many lives lost and ruined because of bin Laden. Maybe some of the grieved will feel some sense of relief now that he's gone. I'm not sure it helps. I'd like to think it does.

I spend the next few hours in front of the TV, myself and the talking heads pouring over the same thoughts about the potential healing effect of his death and parsing through what little information there is at this point about the operation.

I eventually get drowsy, turn off Bruce's TV, and head back to the Failure Cave for a few hours' rest.

By midmorning the details are coming out. It was a SEAL Team Six operation in the dark of night. One of the helicopters had to be destroyed on site because of a crash. Journalists from all over the world, some of which I know, are scrambling to get to\the scene of the raid, a town in Pakistan called Abbottabad.

I pick up where I left off last night, absorbing each nugget in stories posted online until one detail leaps out and fills me with glee.

Apparently one of the SEALs shot bin Laden in the face. In the eye, to be exact.

Don't know if that's healing anyone else's sorrow, but it sure as hell is putting a bounce in my step.

# CHAPTER 26
# AFGHANISTAN OR THE ABYSS

MAY 3, 2011
CORAL GABLES, FLORIDA

The wait is killing me. I check my phone constantly for missed calls and new emails. I won't put it down, even for a moment. I can't. I'm waiting for the call that will determine the course of the rest of my life.

*Ugh! Stop being such a drama queen!*

Worried about how I'll react if I don't like what I hear, I pace up and down the driveway outside the Failure Cave in bare feet, taking gargantuan drags off my American Spirit Light. I've duped myself into believing I'm doing my lungs less harm by smoking these hippy-dippy cigarettes instead of good, old-fashioned, sure-to-give-you-cancer-and-wear-a-hole-in-your-throat Marlboros. I light one off of another, awkwardly cradling my phone in the hand holding my last butt's red-hot cherry against the tip of a fresh one.

The call I'm awaiting is from the editor who will tell me if I'm going back to Afghanistan. Not CBS's Constance Lloyd, who met me at the airport in New York when I first arrived from Germany. Constance already said she won't use me in Afghanistan anymore. That's a bad sign, one of many I've gotten from her and CBS in recent months. Earlier this year, when the protests kicked off to oust Egyptian President Hosni Mubarak, I told Constance I wanted to go. She immediately turned me down, saying I wasn't fit for work because my eye hadn't healed and I still had another surgery to go. Doctors said it was a no-go as well. There was no arguing. I really wanted to be there, even though I was scared that with the bricks and bullets flying at demonstrations—and me with only one working eye—there was good chance I could get clobbered.

I had a personal stake in seeing events unfold in Egypt. It's where I started my career as an overseas reporter back in the late '90s. In those days, my colleagues and I often wondered whether real change would ever come to authoritarian Egypt. Mubarak was a military dictator in an Armani suit, capable of dropping the hammer on any would-be dissenters. He kept Islamic extremists mostly in check for two decades except for a handful of attacks. Still, we figured Egypt just needed a spark to ignite the rest of the populace into demanding change. Our forecasts were only off by a decade or so. In a land whose history stretches back 7,000 years, we were pretty damn close.

I swallowed not going to Egypt for CBS and missing the boat on Libya and Syria. But I've told myself I have to go back to Afghanistan once I'm cleared to work, no matter what.

It's become what I recognize as an unhealthy obsession. Ever since the fog of pain medication lifted and I could raise my head, I've wanted it. Call it the ultimate testament to the endurance of rocks-in-the-head stupidity, but I won't be chased away on someone else's terms, namely the guy who shot me and everyone I know telling me I must have said rocks in my head for wanting to go back. And I refuse to be shooed into a corner, forced to sit at a desk and commit faux acts of journalism for the rest of my career with my dick tucked between my legs because I'm too scared I might get hurt again.

There's only one outlet entertaining the idea of sending me back to Afghanistan. I filed a handful of stories for *USA Today* before I was hurt and during my previous trips there. Foreign editor William Dermody seems to like my stuff and is showing a ridiculous amount of faith in me. They are my only shot right now for going back to Afghanistan. CBS has cut me loose and the other outlets I approached about an assignment said no, with some editors taking pains to question my sanity for wanting to go back.

But William never has. He's the only one who doesn't tell me I'm crazy. Even if he thinks it, he's at least courteous enough not to mention it to me. For weeks, William and I have been going back and forth on the phone and via email about what stories I'd cover and where I'd embed. I've already lined up a few locales in southern and eastern Afghanistan, where most of the fighting typically takes place. All he needs to do is get the OK from the *USA Today* bean counters and I'd be on my way. Apparently there is some debate whether it's worth spending the price of the salary I requested and the expenses I projected for several months of coverage.

Meanwhile the fighting season is already underway. The snow has melted in the mountain passes—the fighters returned from their long winter siestas in hovels in Pakistan and penthouses in Dubai. The action has already ramped up around some of the combat outposts I'm planning to visit. IED placement has increased, harassing gunfire on convoys and foot patrols on the rise. The show has already started. I just need to get my ticket punched.

Adding to my anxiousness was the official end of my eight-month, doctor-ordered journalism hiatus a few days ago. While it was a long-anticipated and welcome day, I'm worried my reporting skills have gone to rot while wasting away these last few months in the Failure Cave. I'm eager to get cracking again to see if I can even still do the job.

It's also a financially frightening prospect. There are no more monthly worker's compensation checks as of May 1. Meager though they were, those payments were sustaining me since I got shot. Without them, and a new assignment, I'll be completely, fiscally fucked in less than a month.

Perhaps even more terrifying than the prospect of living in a cardboard box on the street and foraging through fast food dumpsters for dinner is the notion that I might actually get sent back to Afghanistan. I've told myself I want this more than anything. But now that the prospect of it actually happening is here, just a phone call way, I'm not so sure.

*Stop muddying the waters! You want to go!*

Part of me knows I need to go back for reasons beyond a paycheck. I need to return to Afghanistan if I ever want to be whole again. It's the last place I felt like I mattered. When William said he wanted to send me back he was unwittingly throwing me a much-needed lifeline. In Afghanistan, I would have purpose again.

Being there would mean getting further away from everyone I screwed over here. Some additional distance would do my conscience some good. In all, the thought of fleeing to a familiar war comforts me. I stopped fantasizing about dying and started thinking about what the next few months of reporting might entail. I was scared, though excited.

Initially I thought going back was a done deal until William informed me of the budget concerns. For the last couple of weeks, it's been back and forth several times between "Yes, you're going" and "Not sure we have the money." I told him I needed to know by today.

He promised me an answer.

A part of me wants to go to Afghanistan just so I feel like I have a reason to be, well, alive.

The other is ready to give up, pack it in, wondering how much longer this life has to last for it to be considered one not cut short.

*Really? You're being ridiculous!*

I huff another American Spirit while contemplating a grim, binary reduction of my existence to Afghanistan or The Abyss.

My phone rings.

# PART THREE

I have that terrible itch for the unknown which impels me to undertake all kinds of follies.

—Paul Gauguin

# CHAPTER 27
# I TAKE IT BACK!

MAY 20, 2011
KABUL, AFGHANISTAN

As soon as the wheels touch the runway, I start cursing myself for coming back.

*This is a bad idea, you fucking idiot! You have no business being here!*

My testicles are apparently in agreement, having retreated into my stomach to hide until I come to my senses and catch the next flight out of here. I clench my fists, then shake them out, repeating this over and over as if I'm trying to pump out the fear toxins and paranoia swelling in my gut since the plane took off from Dubai.

*What the fuck are you trying to prove? That you're not afraid?*

*Well, now you're here. Happy?*

Sweat streams down my lower back as the plane taxis toward the terminal. I grab my camera bag and stand in the aisle behind aid workers, contractors, and Afghan families waiting for the ground crew to roll the stairs to the side of the plane. Mid-May in Kabul is usually pleasant. It's warm, but not sweltering. But when I walk down the stairs and step onto the tarmac, it feels like I'm wading in lava. The heat from the black asphalt radiates up my pant legs and grabs my crotch as if to say "Gotcha!"

*I really shouldn't be here, I really shouldn't be here, I really shouldn't be here . . .*

Amid my nonstop, downward spiral of self-doubt, I imagine what would happen if I called William at *USA Today* and told him I changed my mind and was coming home. He'd understand. I bet he wouldn't say a word otherwise. I let this possibility play out in my mind and forecast what would come next for me after aborting an assignment like this.

*That's probably it for you if you pussy out now, you know that, right? No one will ever send you on another assignment. Ever.*

Life as a journalism outcast, never getting another opportunity to do the type of stories I love. I'd probably have to leave the business altogether. And as I'm skilled in little else other than my two previous professions—bouncer at a bar and swim instructor for young children—my options in life are pretty limited. Even then, it might be best I take off now and end my career on an unceremonious note with my tail between my legs. It's better than the alternative scenario running through my head: me on my first embed with US forces in some remote corner of the country, balled up in the fetal position with Taliban bullets whizzing around and crying like a six-year-old whose puppy was run over by a car.

The possibility of that happening hadn't occurred to me while I was lining up several months of embeds with the military in the most tumultuous parts of Afghanistan: Kandahar, Kunar, and Helmand, to name a few of the hot spots I'll visit. But now, with a cyclone of doubt whirling between my ears, I'm starting to wonder whether my failure to forecast this calamity was a result of what psychologists commonly refer to as "defensive avoidance," or outright, padded-room-and-a-bottle-of-lithium delusion. I don't want to step one foot outside the airport, let alone in some rural village controlled by the Taliban waiting to decapitate me for having the gall to come back.

*Get it together! Breathe!*

I compose myself just enough to follow the other passengers to the terminal's passport control. While standing there I try to strike a casual pose that will mask my fear and look around at others, hoping to catch a glimpse of someone showing like-minded terror for support. Noting no others like me, I retreat into my own psychosis, suck in a deep breath, then exhale hard, hoping to force the fear out of me. I do it again, inadvertently blowing my rancid plane breath onto the back of the neck of a middle-aged security contractor in cargo pants and what appears to be a toddler's T-shirt accentuating his formidable biceps.

"My bad," I offer when he turns around and gives me the stink eye. I've got to pull myself together.

*Jeez, I need a cigarette.*

This is perhaps the only place in the country where you can't smoke and it's rigorously enforced.

*Just think about something else.*

My mind drifts to my default distraction when I'm trying not to contemplate my fears. Daydreaming about sex is a time-honored and proven distraction for me and every penis owner. However, the Kabul Airport is perhaps the least inspiring place for erotic imaginings known to man. It's grimly lighted and blandly appointed, as if to subliminally lower visitors' expectations for what the rest of the country has in store. I decide to instead just stare at the back of the contractor's head, breathing through my nose and trying not to panic.

Finally, it's my turn at passport control. The officer does a cursory flip through the pages of my passport, pausing for a moment on the page-sized sticker from El Salvador, then stamps my documents. Through the door and over to the carousel, I pick up my bags, pass through customs unnoticed, and head to the lobby, where dozens of taxi drivers are vying for fares. I try to remain calm amid the melee, waving off one offer after another. I prefer to grab a cab outside the terminal, where it's cheaper.

*You've got this. Just keep moving.*

I flag down one of the less ambitious drivers, load my bags in the back seat, then get in the front. I always ride shotgun in a cab. I think it makes me look less conspicuous, though frankly I'm pretty easy to spot as a foreigner, seeing as I'm about fifty pounds heavier than your average Afghan male and can't grow a very respectable beard.

We pull out of the airport and head into the city, passing roadside stalls selling mufflers, slabs of beef, and cellphone covers. I stare out the window at the bustle on the streets and the mountains in the distance. It's real now.

*This is what you wanted, right? Now you've got it. What are you going to do with it?*

I roll down the window a crack so I can finally smoke a cigarette and take in Kabul. The city has grown considerably since the first time I came here in 2005. These days there's construction everywhere. The influx of development dollars has clearly been good to wealthy Afghans with international connections. There are cranes and construction sites visible on both sides of the main road from the airport. The war has also drawn millions of Afghans out of the countryside into the capital hoping to escape the violence. They come here with nothing, many forced to live in hovels shadowed by construction sites and in crowded refugee camps on the outskirts. I've got to make a point to do some reporting on conditions here between embeds.

Stories about just Afghans, however, are always a tough sell to certain outlets. Most folks at home aren't all that interested in Afghanistan anyway, and stories without American voices rack up even fewer hits online. It's a sad testament to our collective apathy that I try not to dwell on when considering just how few people actually read what I write. If I gave it any serious thought, I probably wouldn't bother to sit down to a keyboard ever again.

My worries about the feeble reach of my work prove just the distraction I needed from my fear as the taxi circles around the monument to Ahmad Shah Massoud, the slain leader of the Northern Alliance who was killed by al Qaeda a day before the September 11 attacks. From there, it's just a short distance to my hotel of choice in Kabul's Wazir Akbar Khan neighborhood. I see nothing's changed around here amid all the growth. The Diana is the same as always, a shabby little guesthouse with a dozen or so rooms surrounded by a concrete wall, on top of which is a watchtower made of corrugated metal. That tower must be a sleep-inducing, brain-baking oven, which would explain the failure of the guard inside it to respond to my efforts to get his attention until my third and loudest greeting of "Salaam al-Alaakum." I then hear the gate latch loosen. The other guard on duty swings it open on squeaky hinges. The muzzle of his AK-47 drags on the ground as he moves aside so I can enter.

I like the Diana. It's low-profile and cheap enough that no one would bother to bomb it because no one of consequence—myself included—ever stays here. I reason its lack of ostentation makes it a safer option than a more luxurious locale. My editors like it because it's cheap. Other hotels take elaborate security precautions. The most expensive hotel in Kabul, the Serena, has a small cadre of well-armed personnel, several layers of security measures, and high walls to protect guests from suicide attacks and mortar fire. Consequently, it is often targeted. But not the good ole' Diana, I tell myself while vigorously knocking on wood.

When I walk into the lobby, the staff greets me warmly and makes no note of my new glasses and ragged facial scar. Their nonchalance is somehow reassuring.

"Hello, Mr. Carmen," says Khaled, the guesthouse's manager, in his sleepy lilt. "It's good to see you. Are you staying with us long?"

I ask Khaled if he has a room, having not booked one in advance. I never do. There's always room at the Diana. Khaled goes through the ritual of checking the books, then asks me to choose among the half a dozen rooms that are free. While I fill out some paperwork, Khaled makes no mention of what happened to me last year, though I'm pretty sure he knows. I'd left a couple bags with him before taking off for Kunar last September. My friend and fellow reporter, Jason Motlagh, was also staying here when I was hurt. He gathered my stuff for me when he heard about my injury. He must have told Khaled.

"You want some breakfast, Mr. Carmen?"

I decline. I'm not hungry, just exhausted from my trans-Atlantic excursion and eight-hour layover in Dubai. It's 8:00 in the morning in Kabul, so midnight back in the States. I'm exhausted but too anxious to rest. I drop my bags in my room, grab my cigarettes, and head for the small garden. I light up and pull deep drags, lost in contemplation of the situation I created, until I smell the filter burn. Then I light another. Following my nicotine courage fortification, I screw myself up to head out the door with a pep talk.

*Stop stalling, you chickenshit. No use dragging your feet. Just go out there.*

The last time I walked through Shar-e-Now Park, a man with a BB gun charged me 50 Afghani, about a dollar, to shoot at some paper targets he'd tacked to a sheet of plywood. My aim was terrible. I missed almost every time from just a few yards away. I hope he's here. I want to see if my mostly monocular view of the world has improved my marksmanship.

I don't see him, but the park is busy today. Young boys lope in a pack along a winding path lined with trees. An emaciated stray dog follows them, nosing for affection, or better yet, some scraps. Women, forbidden during Taliban rule from entering the park alone, are enjoying the urban oasis. It's not much. Shar-e-Now has certainly seen better days. But the park is a much-needed reprieve for residents from Kabul city streets clogged with cars, trucks, and motorbikes, lined with open sewers reeking of excrement. When I'm in this part of town, I always cut through the park to give myself a break from Kabul's chaos and pungent aromas. I had scurried here from the

Diana, not to evade the stench, but to avoid would-be kidnappers, gunmen, and other assorted imagined terrors that have been following me ever since I stepped foot in the country.

But Kabul is a relatively safe city for foreigners. Maybe "safe" is the wrong word. Compared to where I got shot, it's pretty safe. But bad things can, and often do, happen here. When the UN guesthouse near the park was attacked by Taliban suicide gunmen a couple of years ago, I was staying at a hotel even cheaper than the Diana just a few blocks away. A photographer friend and I ran over to cover it and afterward sketched out our own escape plan in the event of an attack on our $20-a-night flophouse. We estimated we could jump from rooftop to rooftop to safety, giggling at the prospect of living out some adolescent parkour fantasy by leaping between tall buildings in a single bound. It was a ridiculous plan predicated on denial of very real dangers, but it made us feel safe. How I long for those days of blissful arrogance. Or perhaps it was sheer stupidity. Either way, I never gave walking through Kabul a second thought, even after a deadly attack like the one we covered.

Today, it terrifies me.

Jason and I had agreed to meet at the Herat Restaurant just off the park. It's a Kabul landmark known for its savory kabobs and other traditional dishes. He's already there when I arrive and hands me a bag of clothes and other gear I'd left at the hotel eight months ago.

"How does it feel to be back?" he asks, eyeing me closely, probably wondering, as I still do, if my being here is such a good idea. Jason has been in and out of Afghanistan for years, having spent more time here than I covering the fighting. We both started out working at the same dysfunctional news wire in DC, which prompted us to plot similar courses leading as far away from the Beltway as possible.

I ask him about the latest news and unfounded gossip on some of the provinces I plan to hit in the coming months. He winces when I mention Kunar, the province where I was shot.

"So you're going back, huh?" He offers a half laugh and looks at me sideways.

I tell him I'm not heading back to PK, but to a combat outpost not far from where I was shot. He shakes his head without saying anything.

"I know, I know," I say, answering the question he never verbalized. "But I don't know . . . I just have to." I quickly switch gears and tell Jason about the recent relationship mishaps that landed me in hot water with two women. He laughs at my predicament, prompting me to do likewise. By the time we're done eating, my face hurts from laughing, and I realize it's probably because I'd done so little smiling of late and that the muscles around my mouth are out of shape. It's a good hurt.

After lunch we part ways. Jason's getting ready to do an embed in the east. I'm headed for the south, to Kandahar Province. We say we'll get together again before we go, though we both know that's not likely. I'm not sure when I'll see him again. I'm just glad I got to spend time with someone who knows me, even if it's only for an hour. I probably see Jason only once a year, if that. It seems like my good friends are always someplace I'm not, which means I'm often lonely. And not just these last few months in my Miami exile. But always. There's an inherent loneliness that comes from seeing and experiencing things the vast majority of people never will. Some folks might ask you about it, but as soon as you start talking, their eyes glaze over, signaling you to stop so they can resume their lives of willful ignorance, unfettered by the many downers this world has to offer. Maybe I'm just sad to see my friend go.

I watch Jason walk down the street half a block before turning and heading back to the Diana. Suddenly I'm exhausted. I drag myself back to the hotel and stumble headfirst into my sunken, misshapen mattress and fall into a deep sleep without bothering to turn off the lights.


I dream of dryness. A dusty breeze. My throat parched and coarse. In the distance I hear a guttural heaving. A regular cadence. Then something wakes me. Just my head comes up at the neck.

*Where am I?*

Happens every time I travel this far: "Jetlag Amnesia." I look around and notice the room's heavy maroon drapes and clunky furniture. I always forget where I am after my first sleep in Afghanistan. Then it comes back to me in a rush. I try falling back to sleep, but can't because I'm so thirsty. I chug what's left in my water bottle. Must have been snoring, loudly, if I heard it in my dreams.

I look at my phone. It reads eight o'clock. Morning or night? Darkness outside—so night. I have three missed calls in quick succession, the last was just a few minutes ago. I call back. It's a sergeant with military public affairs informing me I have to be at Bagram Airfield in the morning to catch a flight to Kandahar Province, where I'll link up with a unit on the frontier of the US troop surge in a traditional Taliban stronghold. I wasn't expecting this. Not so soon. Typically it takes a few days for them to find a seat for media. Journalists are the lowest priority on the totem pole and are accommodated only when there's empty seats on the aircraft unless it's a network bigwig like Brian Williams or anyone from *60 Minutes*. For them, there are always seats.

I've got to be out there early in the morning. I arrange for a car to pick me up at 6:00 tomorrow morning and drive me the hour and change it takes from the capital to Bagram, NATO's hub in the east. I lie back in my bed, hoping to doze some more so I'm rested for tomorrow's travel and the official beginning of my assignment. I start thinking about how very soon I'll be back in the company of soldiers, amid a local populace that could very well contain someone eager to target a frightened reporter who the Taliban neglected to kill the first time.

I'm still awake thinking of that possibility when my alarm goes off at 5:30 the next morning, just enough time for a quick shower before my ride gets here.

# CHAPTER 28
# FEAR SWEAT AND CELINE DION

MAY 28, 2011
COMBAT OUTPOST GHUNDY GHAR, KANDAHAR PROVINCE, AFGHANISTAN

Capt. Daniel Sundberg is listening to a couple of Afghan farmers who came to this tiny combat outpost in Taliban territory to ask him for money. Speaking through an interpreter, they allege that a nearby road commissioned by the US military cut through their fields, causing them to lose a portion of their yield and significant income. While airing their grievances, a couple of Sundberg's guys eyeball the Afghan men suspiciously. It's not their story raising red flags— claims of lost property are not uncommon. Some of the guys think one of the farmers resembles an insurgent who escaped custody in a recent mass prison break orchestrated by the Taliban.

To find out one way or the other, the soldiers pull out a device that scans irises and fingerprints, then compares them to a database of features belonging to suspected insurgents and convicts in Afghanistan. It's high-tech wizardry in the land that time forgot (locals here still pull their water out of a well dug by the Persians centuries ago). No matches to known escapees or bad guys turn up. However, Sundberg's men discover that one of the Afghan farmers, Fazil Ahmed, had previously been paid $800 in damages for the road's bisection of an irrigation canal that waters rows and rows of grapevines that thrive here despite Kandahar's scorching summer heat. Sneaky, sneaky.

"Why did you lie to me?" Sundberg asks the men, who have the look of a couple of kids caught stealing candy bars from the corner store. "I don't know why you didn't tell me up-front. You hurt my feelings!"

The captain's men struggle to maintain straight faces while Sundberg berates the would-be con men for trying to pull a fast one. I stifle my own laughter while scribbling the exchange in my notebook and write "lede?" at the top of the page, a note to myself that I might make this unintentionally comical, yet telling, exchange the starting point of my first story from the Afghan front in eight months.

I arrived at Combat Outpost Ghundy Ghar a few days ago. Getting here took a while. The wait at Bagram for a seat to open on a flight to Kandahar Airfield was only two days. That's pretty quick. I've been stuck in some places for a week or more. Once I got to "KAF," as the airfield in Kandahar is commonly known, I had another few days to cool my heels while waiting for a seat on a helicopter that would take me to an even smaller base. While there, I bide my time interviewing an Australian general about efforts to train Afghan forces to take over the country's security and do a piece about the video gaming habits of soldiers. *USA Today* likes when I mix in the occasional slice-of-life piece with the reporting I do on embeds. This also gives me an opportunity to warm up my pen a bit before heading out. It's been so long since I've done any reporting or writing. At first the words come slowly, spilling onto the page in clumsy phrases. It takes me half a day to write up the short piece on what type of video games soldiers prefer: first-person shoot 'em ups versus sports.

The night before I'm scheduled to depart KAF for my embed, I get a note from William, my editor. He wants me to write a piece to go with a video interview of me that was shot at *USA Today* headquarters right before I traveled to Afghanistan. I went to the home office in McLean, Virginia, a gleaming, mirrored tower in the DC suburbs that looks more like the corporate headquarters of Blue Cross/Blue Shield than a news outfit, to pick up some new body armor and a helmet. I showed a video editor the piece Brian had put together from the footage I shot of my injury. He asked if he could use it alongside an on-camera interview with me. I agreed to do it even though I am self-conscious about the way my eye looks. The lid is still sagging and my pupil hasn't contracted as much as I'd hoped, allowing in way more light than I'd like. I can't be without my sunglasses when outdoors, even for a moment. I'd wear them inside if I could, but one needs the cachet of someone like Jack Nicholson to pull off that look.

William emails me the video and asks that I write a piece recalling what happened, a first-person narrative that "puts readers at the scene." I watch the cut, skimming over the part where I'm hit. I've still only seen that the one time at Brian's, which was more than enough. I watch myself recall that day in the village, slouched in a chair and appearing somewhat pudgy. All that stewing in The Failure Cave apparently packed a few pounds around my middle and put a curve in my spine.

I sit down to type, wondering whether William realizes that asking me to recount my worst day the night before heading out on my first embed since getting shot is tantamount to psychological torture. I silently curse him, knowing he means no harm. Still, I'm irked.

*Why not waterboard me and pull out my fingernails while you're at it? I'm already scared out of my fucking mind! Are you trying to push me over the edge?*

I step away from my laptop and head outside to pace in circles and chain-smoke, then return to my room, sit down, and start angrily mashing the keys until I produce a reasonable recollection of what happened.

The next morning I'm flown to a small base by helicopter and link up with a convoy of armored vehicles heading to Ghundy Ghar. My first time outside the wire is a scrotum-tightening terror. The trucks travel a stretch of dirt road known for its abundance of IEDs. During the entire ride I kept eyeing the floor of the vehicle, wondering when its steel-plated floorboards would burst open in jagged sheets and shear off both my legs.


Ghundy Ghar sits on a lone hilltop surrounded for miles by farmer fields and the occasional cluster of mud and brick homes, making it the perfect vantage point for observing the locals and the occasional Taliban fighter in their midst. It's in Kandahar's Zharay District, not far from the birthplace of the Taliban's spiritual leader: the one-eyed Mullah Omar.

Legend has it that this hilltop was constructed by Alexander the Great's men, who defeated the local tribes of Afghanistan in the 4th century BC

While I'm skeptical of the veracity of this tale of ancient engineering, I do enjoy the fantastic 360-degree view the hill affords of the rows of grapevines, poppy stalks left standing from the recent opium harvest, and wheat.

Aesthetics aside, having the high ground is also a tactical advantage. Most soldiers in this part of Afghanistan have to deal with the Taliban at eye level. Up here, there is no chance anyone is going to sneak up on them and even less of getting pounded by mortar fire.

Many of the locals living around Ghundy Ghar are still getting used to the full-time presence of US and Afghan troops in their neighborhood. Rumor has it that when American soldiers first came through here, some of the locals thought they were Soviet troops returning to reclaim Ghundy Ghar, which the Soviets lost to the Mujahideen. The Mujahideen were clandestinely armed by the United States in their fight against the Soviets; many would later become the Taliban, thus making the hilltop outpost a physical embodiment of the perpetual loop of violence that has plagued Afghanistan for the last few decades.

It'd be comic if so many innocent people hadn't died in the process.


Sundberg and his men from the 10th Mountain Division have been in-country less than two months, but they're already well-versed in locals' efforts to hit them up for compensation a second, even third time. Attempting to bilk the Army out of an extra buck or two is not uncommon. And who could blame them? Millions of largely unaccounted dollars trade hands every day in a woefully impoverished country with no visible means of supporting itself and next to no government oversight. If I were those farmers, I'd try to squeeze a hell of a lot more than a few hundred bucks from Uncle Sam. But I'm not nearly as crafty or brazen as the two who slunk out empty-handed, presumably to try their luck at the next combat outpost.

Con men are the least of their concerns here. The villages around Ghundy Ghar are thick with Taliban fighters that easily slip in and out of the towns by night and prowl the pitch-black fields planting IEDs and stockpiling weapons and explosives. Some of the locals are still on the fence about who they'd rather have ruling the roost: the Taliban, who they have been forced to tolerate, and in some cases fully support; or the Americans, who offer financial aid to build roads, irrigation canals, and schools, but sometimes, accidentally, shoot and kill civilians.

These young men—along with a handful of female soldiers—at Ghundy Ghar are tasked with convincing locals to get on board with their anti-Taliban agenda. It'd be a near impossible task for a well-resourced, seasoned diplomat used to dealing with the most stubborn of opponents, but for a young commander and company of 20-somethings hoping to stay alive and unscathed, it's a monumental challenge that's just beginning as the fighting season heads into full swing.

I don't envy their job.

"They know they can come here to discuss their problems, but they say they are afraid to get too close to us because the Taliban come to the villages at night," Sundberg tells me. I write this down, shaking the rust off my reporting skills that had laid dormant for so long. It feels good to work after months of wondering whether I'll have the stones to get back into it. No time to pat myself on the back though. I'm still sweating the idea of heading out on a patrol with the guys who walk these roads and fields every day. I'm already unnerved by Sundberg's description of the situation here and the amount of Taliban in the area.

I try not to show my fear in front of him. Instead, I tell the young captain I'm considering leading my story with his exchange with the farmers to exemplify the challenges he and his men face trying to figure out who's a friend and who's a foe. It's a distinction that can change day to day, if not hour to hour, in Afghanistan; the tribal elder with whom you're drinking tea in the morning sometimes tells the Taliban what you talked about that afternoon.

He winces at the idea of me relating his awkward exchange and schoolboy admonishing of the farmers. I tell him it will endear him to readers and reel them into the story with an amusing anecdote. I don't know why I say this. Usually I never let subjects know how I plan to write about them. I need to lock it up and get my head straight. It's been a while. My assertion convinces him that my tact for the story will prove amusing.

"Great. I'll never hear the end of it now," he laughs. Then before I leave, Sundberg reminds me to be ready at 0900 to link up with the platoon going on patrol.

I swallow hard and tell him I won't be late.

Another platoon has just come back from a patrol, so I head over to their barrack to talk to them. Things are starting to heat up around Ghundy Ghar now that the poppy crop has been harvested, marking the start of the fighting season. The Taliban taxes the locals on their yield, the profits of which help fund their fight. So far, none of Sundberg's troops have been seriously injured, although six IEDs have exploded near one unlucky platoon during patrols over the past two months.

During a recent patrol, Pfc. Adolfo Cavazos was walking the point, sweeping back and forth along a dirt path with his ground-penetrating radar, when an IED exploded right beneath him, sending him flying through the air.

"Only part of it blew," the twenty-year-old says with the nonchalance of a recent teenager who knows he's indestructible. He tells me his back hurts a little, as if he strained it shooting hoops.

"If the whole thing had gone off, I wouldn't be here."

I know that feeling. I wish I could be as cavalier about my own close call as the youngster.

After interviewing Cavazos and a few other guys, I head up to Ghundy Ghar's highest ridge to visit the Afghan forces stationed here. Earlier in the day they had a flag-raising ceremony for their enormous national banner that flies on a makeshift pole braced with numerous guide wires. It was a symbolic gesture of their supposed willingness to one day assume full responsibility for security from American forces in this corner of Kandahar.

Now they're resting in their barracks to escape the scorching, midday sun. Their housing stands in stark contrast to the American quarters, what with their neat rows of cots in massive tents shaped like half a cylinder on its side with air-conditioning so cold you can see your breath. The Afghans, meanwhile, have no such comforts in their rough-hewn accommodations. Theirs are huts made of plywood, with windowless holes to let the occasional dust-filled breeze pass through these foul-smelling, dark hovels. Plywood bunks line each of the long walls of the narrow barracks, cramming as many soldiers into one building as possible. Some of the bunks have filthy mattresses. Others, only a blanket. It's more POW camp than living quarters, but these are typical accommodations for Afghan soldiers. I've actually seen worse.

Despite their few comforts, the Afghan soldiers at Ghundy Ghar are receiving good marks from their US counterparts, who are tasked with training them. But concerns remain about their preparedness and professionalism. Getting the Afghan forces ready to take over from NATO forces is the primary objective these days. And it's proving a real bitch.

While on patrol, the Afghans don't like to wear their helmets. They complain they're too cumbersome. The soldiers sport mismatched uniforms and wrap scarves around their heads. Their heavy gunners crisscross belts of ammo across their chest like Mexican banditos in a spaghetti western. It's admittedly a very cool look, though wholly impractical when the shooting starts.

When shots do ring out, the Afghans turn their weapons in the direction of the attack and fire their AK-47s and other weapons until they've exhausted all their ammo, a tactic commonly referred to as "spray and pray." Afghan Army Lt. Hasib Higran tells me what his men lack in experience they make up for in enthusiasm for the mission.

"I just want to remove all enemies from Afghanistan and help bring peace," he tells me over a lunch of rice, kabobs, and fresh bread in his officers' barracks, a small trailer with one electrical outlet for a desk lamp and TV. That night, I join him after dinner to talk again and watch an Afghan version of an amateur singing competition modeled after those in America. And like Americans sitting at home, shoving Cool Ranch Doritos into their bloated, apathetic pie holes, we laugh at the ineptitude and willingness of others to humiliate themselves publicly for a few moments in the spotlight.

"Someday we'll be ready to defend this country ourselves, God willing," he says following his latest fit of laughter.

The next morning, as I'm preparing to head out on my first foray into the Afghan wild since being shot in the face, I look up the hill toward the Afghan camp and notice the top half of the pole has collapsed under the weight of the massive flag. It's cloaking the half dozen Afghan soldiers scrambling underneath it to keep the emblem of their national pride from touching the ground.


The pre-mission brief is something I've heard hundreds of times. Lieutenants and first sergeants go over the mission objective and everyone's responsibility in the event of an IED, small arms fire, or a complex attack combining both coupled with rocket fire for good measure. There was a time when I would zone out during the briefs or take the opportunity to shoot some footage of soldiers standing in a circle smoking cigarettes, looking pensive. For me it was old hat, akin to the preflight instructions given by some overworked flight attendant you ignore while perusing the selection of Harry Potter wands in the SkyMall catalogue.

But not this time.

This time I listen with rapt attention to the mission objective. The platoon, along with their Afghan Army partners, will patrol the nearby grape field and head over to a small village to see if they can locate one of the village's elders.

The first sergeant comes up to me and instructs me on what to do in the event I'm hit or blown up. "Stay down. Don't move. A medic will come to you." Nothing I haven't heard, except this time it sounds like the preamble to a death sentence handed down by the grim reaper himself. Rivers of fear sweat course down my back and sides. The blubbering in my brain is nearing physical manifestation in real tears as we head out the main gate and navigate the narrow, dusty road toward the grape rows. We walk single file to lessen the possibility of triggering any IEDs laying in wait. I take great pains to step in the exact same place as the man in front of me while trying to film the column of soldiers.

*Well, you wanted to be "whole." Congratulations on conquering your fears and contradicting everyone who insisted you shouldn't be here. You showed them who's not afraid to walk through a mine-strewn field. Hope you're happy.*

The Afghan forces are seemingly less concerned about being blown up. They meander off the line laid out by the minesweeper at the head of the patrol. We head for the fields, walking up and down row after row of grapes in stifling 100-plus degree heat, made worse by the humidity pulsating off the vines. It feels like we're marching through split pea soup. At the end of each row there is a waist-high mud wall that we climb over one at a time. The walls are a favorite hiding place for Taliban explosives in hopes of blasting some unlucky soldier's balls off.

We climb over several of the walls without incident and head to a nearby village to speak with some locals. I lurk on the periphery at first, hoping to remain clear of the blast radius of any would-be suicide bombers with enough explosives to take out an entire platoon single-handedly. Everything that can go wrong is going to go wrong right now. I can feel it. I'm getting that hinky feeling I had when I got shot. Something's not right here. A man on a motorcycle rides back and forth in the distance, watching the platoon leader talk to a shop owner. I'm convinced we've walked into trap.

*Stay calm. Don't panic. Stay alert.*

I take a deep breath, then go up to the soldiers exchanging pleasantries with the shop owner and other local men that have gathered to see what's happening. I ask the locals about the Taliban threat in the area. They tell me through the platoon's Afghan interpreter that the militants make the villages around Ghundy Ghar their personal playground at night, moving explosives and weapons through the grape rows to huts where they hide their caches. Same thing I heard from the Americans. I scribble in my notebook. Large drops of sweat plop on the pages, smearing the ink.

As we're preparing to leave, a man walks up to a group of us holding a circular device with wires jutting out of it.

*Oh fuck. I knew it. We're goners.*

I'm just about to jump behind a wall for cover from the impending blast when he flicks a switch and the device emits a sappy Celine Dion song. The would-be explosive is a homemade MP3 player he crafted out of spare parts from a cellphone and a smoke detector like some goddamn Afghan MacGyver. I'm both extremely impressed and embarrassed.


Having survived the Celine Dion attack with my balls in my throat and my pride nowhere in sight, we head back to Ghundy Ghar. I review my notes from the first embed, foot patrol reporting I've done in eight months. I'm still petrified beyond comprehension, though trying not to show it in front of the soldiers. I head back to the tent, dig my cigarettes out of my bag—I'm up to a pack a day since arriving in-country—and suck down three in a row while looking at my video footage from the day's patrol. I review the seemingly mundane walk through rows of grapes and scan for piles of fresh-shoveled dirt or errant wires I might have missed that indicate an IED is buried there. Surely there were.

This obsessing isn't helping. I turn off the camera and go to the top of Ghundy Ghar to watch the sun set over poppy fields now barren, their crops cultivated and processed into heroin being injected into the forearms of junkies the world over. Pondering the poppy, I tell myself there are greater worries out here than my own selfish concerns about being blown up. I'm just a visitor passing through their sunbaked nightmare for a week or so. These soldiers will be here for a year; some might not make it home. The locals live with the fear of Taliban tyranny every day of their lives. My fears are small and petty compared to the realities of the dangers faced by others.

*Suck it up and stop moaning, even if it's only to yourself.*

I smoke the last cigarette in the pack while wrestling with these thoughts, then open a fresh one.

*If the IEDs and gunfire don't get me, cancer surely will.*

# CHAPTER 29
# WHACK-A-MOLE WARFARE

JUNE 2, 2011
FORWARD OPERATING BASE PASAB, KANDAHAR PROVINCE, AFGHANISTAN

A colonel tells me my fifteen-minute interview with the general is scheduled for the end of the day. That is, if he has any time after visiting a nearby school the Taliban previously shut down, followed by an in-depth briefing from every US commander in southeast Afghanistan.

Frankly, I'm not all that keen on doing the interview, but when the opportunity arises to talk to Gen. David Petraeus, commander of all NATO forces in Afghanistan, I know I can't turn up my nose. My editors really want it. Petraeus is a name most readers recognize from the Iraq war and, in the minds of some, he's the 21st century's Gen. Patton.

Not mine, but some.

Personally, I don't much like talking to "top brass" like Petraeus. Their answers are too polished. Everything they say is a well-rehearsed sound bite that puts positive spin on even the direst of situations.

Part of me can't blame him for trying to put a sunny sheen on the war, especially after the whole Gen. McChrystal/*Rolling Stone* debacle, when the general bad-mouthed members of the Obama administration to a reporter, prompting in his resignation.

But unlike free-wheeling, hip-shooting McChrystal, Petraeus is more akin to the CEO of a large corporation who will say anything while imploring the shareholders—in this case, the American public—to hang in there for the promised upswing in the company's fortunes even though the stock is currently taking a colossal dump.

That's why I see no real value in talking to Petraeus. It's not like he's going to give me anything remotely resembling an honest assessment from his top-rung vantage point. And certainly not in fifteen minutes at the end of a busy day.

Also, it really irks me how the top brass are treated. Generals are received like rock stars. And Petraeus, being the big cheese of the whole Afghanistan enchilada, is like Mick Jagger with a chest full of medals. When he first arrived at Pasab, the first thing I noticed was how his handlers and hangers-on all sported glazed looks of infatuation while observing Petraeus or even talking about him.

I usually have no interest in that malarkey. Most of my stories are about soldiers doing the actual fighting. Sure, I'll throw in a quote from the brigade commander or the occasional major just so my editors think they're getting a "well-rounded story." But for the meat of my reporting, I stick to one rule: keep it to captains or lower. Young enlisted and officers and of course the Afghans are the ones out here doing the real day-to-day fighting. They know a hell of lot more about how the war is going.

Knowing I'm betraying my principles, I spend a few minutes silently pouting while gathering up my body armor and cameras.

*Stop whining, you baby! There's no getting around it.*


I tag along with Petraeus and his entourage to the nearby school, a handful of rooms packed with boys learning lessons by rote repetition scrawled on dusty, smudged blackboards. The general is congenial while talking with the teachers and students. He shakes hands with the youngsters and asks them through his interpreter if they enjoy going to school. I try to find something to take away from this sideshow for my article, but get nothing worthy of inclusion in the small space I'll be allotted for this piece in the newspaper. I snap a few frames of Petraeus walking outside with the school's director, but the midday sun is too bright, and my photographic skills too sorely lacking, for me to get a decent shot.

We head back to base, where the briefing room is prepared for a meeting of all the top commanders in the region. In front of every seat is a Styrofoam box containing a crab salad sandwich, apparently a favorite of Petraeus. The food has been sitting out for a couple of hours, I'm told, in anticipation of the general's scheduled meeting much earlier in the day. I push aside the container in front of me.

*I've already had diarrhea this month, thank you very much.*

While everyone settles in, one of the general's aides informs me that I can sit in on the meeting, but am strictly forbidden from taking notes. However, I notice a fellow civilian situated next to Petraeus with a notebook open and already scribbling. When I inquire who she is and why she can cover the briefing and I can't, the young major rolls his eyes, the apparent lone dissenter among this hoard that hasn't drunk the Petraeus Kool-Aid.

"That's Paula Broadwell. She has special access," he says, adding that she is working with the general on his memoir.

At first I'm irked that I can't include anything from this high-level briefing in my story, but after a few minutes of listening to commanders drone on about their successes in this highly volatile part of the country, I let go of my anger. The way they describe how effective they've been in suppressing the Taliban threat over the last few weeks makes me wonder what any of us are doing here. According to their progress reports, this war is all but in the bag.

*Wait, if that's the case, can we all go home?*

There's no denying that the addition of thousands of troops in Kandahar Province has forced the Taliban out of their traditional strongholds. But it's a "Whack-a-Mole" victory at best. Knock the Taliban down in one area, they pop up in another. The Taliban gets its ears pinned back here in Zharay District, they scurry across the Arghandab River to Panjwai District and set up shop there. The commanders present their successes to Petraeus as decisive blows that will rid Afghanistan of the Taliban forever, or rather, just long enough to keep them from mounting large-scale attacks on US forces other than the occasional truck bomb at the gate of a base, IEDs, sniper fire, and of course the occasional insider threat from Taliban infiltrators into the ranks of the Afghan Army, resulting in the slaying of unsuspecting NATO soldiers who are training the Afghans to take over this hot mess when they eventually leave.

If NATO forces leave as scheduled in a few years from now, it's going to be up to the Afghan forces to keep the Taliban from returning to power, a dicey proposition for a well-trained and armed military force, let alone one comprised of new recruits who are often ill-equipped and underfed. Of course, none of this comes up during successive reports to Petraeus about how well everything is going.

Just as I find myself nodding off amid the seemingly endless self-congratulations, the briefing ends. The general's minder walks me over to a raised platform where Petraeus, several inches shorter than I, has positioned myself so I'm looking up to him. I'm told I have the fifteen minutes promised, no time for extended pleasantries. I pull out my recorder and get right into it with questions about the recent increase in violence in the south, which coincides every year with the return of the warmer weather. Spring and summer are the fighting seasons in Afghanistan. Come October, the mountain passes become snowed in, forcing both sides to put off most of the hostilities for the return of warmer days. I've got myself geared up to hit the general with some tough questions about the resilience of the Taliban this fighting season and the continuing challenges US and NATO forces face while training their Afghan counterparts to one day bear sole responsibility for all of Afghanistan's security.

"While we have a spring offensive going, the Taliban also has a spring offensive and we have seen the Taliban try to carry out sensational attacks and in some cases successively . . . " the general tells me this in a carefully practiced tempo without halting for a breath, likely rehearsed to make it difficult to ask any follow-up questions. His cadence is steady and determined like a locomotive. Petraeus is said to run ten miles every morning, so he's got the lungs to go on for several minutes, eating up half my allotted time with one question. When he finally finishes his answer, I can barely recollect the specifics of what he just said.

*Jesus! This guy is going to do some damage in Washington once he's done here.*

I try to counter his rhetoric with more targeted questions that requires specific answers, hopefully one that begins with a "Yes" or "No."

"If the victories since the arrival of thousands of additional American troops have been so substantial, can a drawdown of US forces be expected in the near future?" I ask, hoping Petraeus will give me something I couldn't copy from a press release.

"The recent progress here is fragile and reversible," he starts out, a recent sound bite I've read him spew to other reporters.

*Damnit!*

He continues with more of the same regarding the handover of security responsibilities to Afghan forces and a scheduled drawdown of US troops later this summer. I try to interject midstream, asking about the possibility of troops staying on in particular provinces where the Taliban are most entrenched. For a moment, he stares me down for having the audacity to interrupt him mid-pontification, then continues at a quicker pace, seemingly anticipating my eagerness to get into another topic.

I ask him about the death of Osama bin Laden just weeks earlier. I don't want to, but my editors requested it specifically. Al Qaeda isn't really a factor in the fight in southern Afghanistan and hasn't been for a long time. But generals and Washington like to keep the al Qaeda narrative a prominent feature of the Afghanistan story so Americans still think they are a threat over here, thus justifying the ongoing fight against the Taliban and other militant groups in Afghanistan, which frankly the US didn't give two shits about, even while the Taliban was harboring bin Laden. That is, until September 11, 2001.

"We want to ensure that Afghanistan does not become an attractive alternative to them again, a safe haven in which they might plot attacks such as those of 9/11," says Petraeus.

And with that planned answer, my allotted time with him is up. I hastily toss in another inquiry about Afghan police forces, to which he replies at length without really answering my question. Afterward, I listen to it three times and can't make headway of what the hell he meant, even though I nodded throughout his answer.

I berate myself for dropping the ball.

*You dumbass!*

I feel dirty and duped. Even worse, I'm mad at myself for squandering the opportunity, even if I didn't want it. Petraeus handed me my ass in that interview, using his apparent Jedi-like ability to ramble at will while I sat in stupefied silence like some slow-witted lackey guarding the gate at Jabba the Hutt's pleasure palace, letting Luke Skywalker saunter right into the throne room.

I write up my notes, but it's neither pleasant nor easy. Despite having little to really "report," I'm slowed by the sudden onset of flu-like symptoms. A chill comes over me even though it's 100-plus degrees outside this time of year. By the time I finish the story I'm near death, shivering and sweating while hacking up a lung. After I email it to my editor, I drag myself to my tent, crawl onto my cot, and zip my sleeping bag up to my neck hoping to doze it off.

I feel better in the morning—must have been one of those 24-hour Afghanistan intestinal illnesses that typically strike me every month or so—I'm also less chagrined by what happened with Big Kahuna. Yes, I felt dirty and disenchanted with my work. But I can't be sour for long. I'm still too damn happy to finally be back doing something I love.

# CHAPTER 30
# TRAILHEAD TO A DEAD END

JUNE 10, 2011
BAGRAM AIRFIELD, PARWAN PROVINCE, AFGHANISTAN

I return to Bagram slightly sleeker—my pants no longer cut into my waist—following my post-Petraeus interview intestinal illness that had me firing out of both ends. Several days of fever, vomiting, and explosive diarrhea shrunk some of the blubber that had collected in rolls and handles around my midsection during my exile in The Failure Cave.

I'm back here waiting for an open seat on another flight that will take me east for my next few embeds. Until then, I've got a few days to kill and make use of my time lining up interviews for another piece I'm working on. It's a story about eye injuries sustained in combat and how they are treated at American military hospitals. I already got most of what I needed while at Kandahar Airfield, interviewing both eye physicians and patients.

I met one young American soldier recovering from a recent attack that came dangerously close to permanently damaging both of his eyes. I wrote his quotes right after we talked, deciding it would lead my piece:

**KANDAHAR AIRFIELD, Afghanistan—Spc. Joshua Pederson was manning his armored vehicle's revolving gun turret when insurgents peppered the hulking truck with rocket-propelled grenades and small arms fire.**

When a round penetrated the vehicle, Pederson said he ducked inside and was hit with fragments and debris that sprayed his face and torso.

Lying in a hospital bed, a Purple Heart freshly pinned to his gown, the 24-year-old Phoenix native bore numerous scabs and sutures along his jaw line and on his eyelids. Small particles of debris had entered his eyes, though they were largely protected thanks to the ballistic-proof glasses he was wearing.

"My eyesight was blurry, but I was able to keep fighting," Pederson recalled with pupils dilated from the drops given to him by eye doctors at Kandahar Regional Military Hospital.

"I got really lucky," he said about his vision, which doctors said would be fine in a few days. He will be ready to return to duty in a couple of weeks . . .

I banged out this opening anecdote, thinking about Pederson's good fortune as well as my own. We're both lucky to be alive and have both of our eyes, though my bad one is bothering me a lot these last few days. Still, at least I have it.

My doctors in New York told me on several occasions that I would have lost my eye had the ophthalmologist at Bagram that repaired my ruptured globe not done such a good job. Their repeated praise of his handiwork is part of the reason why I decided to write this story.

The other reason is personal: I want to see the bed where I woke up after my surgery here, the place where my own road to recovery started.

Some memories of my days at the Bagram hospital are vivid and haunting. I thought about them often while I was recovering in the States. But others are cloaked in a peripheral fog I attribute to head trauma and potent pain medication. When I try to think back to certain details—what the room looked like where I was lying or the color of my gown—it's like I'm trying to make out the china pattern at the bottom of a bowl of chili.

I'd been planning a return to the hospital since I got the green light for this assignment. I didn't tell William it was on my agenda. I figured he wouldn't balk at me writing a story about eye injuries considering my intimate knowledge of the subject. It's also one of the few stories I haven't seen covered here, though I'm certain after a decade of war inspiring millions of stories, someone, somewhere, has already done it.

I head over to the hospital to meet with Air Force Maj. Lisa Mihora, an ophthalmologist. She wasn't in-country when I was shot, but she's heard of my injury, one that is apparently famous among the eye doctors here.

"I know all about you," she tells me, smiling as she recalls how she first heard of my unusual injury from her predecessor, Dr. Darrell Baskin, the physician who operated on me. Baskin is back in the States now, and I ask for his email, telling her I owe him a long overdue "Thank you."

Before we get down to the business of interviewing soldiers and civilians, Mihora offers to give me a checkup, which I gladly accept considering my eye has been redder than usual these last few weeks and like clockwork starts hurting late each day. I figure the persistent dust and diesel fumes from all the generators on bases are the likely cause. The light in Afghanistan isn't helping either. The intense summer sun here is painful for me, particularly when I'm shooting video and photos and can't wear my sunglasses. I keep my bad eye shut when I shoot and compensate for the loss of sight by constantly scanning back and forth. I tell myself this monocular view is what makes me ultra-aware of my surroundings and as such much safer, a lie I believe only while attempting to remain calm outside the wire.

I sit in the examination chair while Mihora checks the pressure in my bad eye just as Dr. Schiff had done in his office in New York. She inserts the blunt end of an instrument into my eye that gently presses the eyeball. I hate this procedure immensely. Though I've been though it so many times, I've never grown accustomed to the goose-bump-inducing discomfort it causes and the sickening feeling of a foreign object pressing against my fragile globe.

Elevated pressure could mean the eye is infected. Low pressure would indicate my eyeball is leaking the jelly giving an eye its shape that came spilling out when I was shot. That would be the more serious of the two diagnoses. Lucky for me, it's the former, Mihora says. To reduce the pressure and infection, she gives me drops to cleanse the eye and reminds me to come back for a checkup the next time I'm in Bagram. I secretly delight in the fact that I'm receiving free, quality follow-up care and medication on the taxpayers' dime, not to mention last year's surgery, which would have set me back the price of a Porsche had I paid for it.

*Thank you, my fellow Americans.*

After my exam, I do a quick interview with Mihora and a member of the Afghan Local Police who suffered a serious eye injury in a grenade attack. Noor Mohammed has a bandage over his right eye reminiscent of the one I wore during my brief tenure here. He tells me the doctors' prognosis for him was similar to mine when I first woke up: that he will probably lose his eye. I try bolstering his spirits, telling him doctors said the same to me, though pull up short of saying he'll be just fine, not wanting to fill him with false hope. I take a few photos of Noor sitting on the floor of the hospital waiting room and wish him luck.

Having completed my journalistic duties, I ask Mihora to show me the ward where I recuperated after my surgery. She walks me over to a nurses' station, which is unfamiliar to me. I'm certain I never ventured this far when I was here. I don't remember making it more than a few steps from my bed to pee in a bottle every few hours.

From there, I walk through a swinging door and enter a room bleached by fluorescent light. It's lined with ten beds, five on each side, separated with curtains, not unlike any hospital stateside. There, in the far right-hand corner, against the back wall, is my bed. There's someone in it. A female in a gown. I assume she's military. She looks fine. Two arms, two legs. No telling what's wrong with her.

She's sitting up, talking to a woman in uniform sitting on her bed. They're sharing a sandwich. I walk over, passing beds with soldiers trying to rest and others with the curtains drawn.

"This used to be my bed," I tell them, immediately realizing I sound like a six-year-old asserting ownership over his toy truck in the sandbox. They stare back at me blankly, possibly wondering where this awkward interruption is headed. I start mumbling a reason for wanting to see the bed, then trail off.

I can't adequately explain to them why I'm here—I often have difficulty admitting it to myself.

For the last month I've been busy with work, once again doing what I love. Writing stories is all I've ever wanted out of a "career." In college, I coined a somewhat vague mantra for what I hoped my future to hold. "I want to see the world and have writing pay the way," I would repeat between bong hits whenever anyone asked me what someone studying philosophy and Arabic was planning for employment. It was an aspiration only a delusional optimistic—and perpetually inebriated—young man could proclaim with a straight face.

Perhaps I would have been better served had I narrowed my travel and writing aspirations to covering warm-climate getaways. But that wasn't what I wanted. Then, just as now, I wanted to go places I shouldn't and do things others wouldn't dare. But in those days my dreams weren't focused on current events. I was hardly aware of what was going on the in the world. Massacres in Somalia and the US response—I'd heard something about it. Genocide in Rwanda—not even on my radar.

But I wanted something that pumped my blood, a risk greater than those I was already taking on a regular basis to procure my most unsavory drug of choice. Part of the allure of heroin during my college days was in not only consuming a potentially fatal narcotic but in going to a notoriously dangerous North Philadelphia neighborhood to score it. Some of my friends wouldn't make the trip to the corner of Eighth Street and Tioga Avenue, one of the best spots for smack. I, on the other hand, liked to go. Heading down there late at night, navigating side streets so potholed you couldn't drive quicker than a crawl, excited me. Some dealers took pains to intimidate naive-looking college kids and often tried to rip us off.

Once, while scoring with my friend Chris, who drove us down there, a dealer smashed his driver-side window with the butt of his gun. I was facing the opposite direction, negotiating with another dealer at my window, when I heard the glass shatter and felt the shards hit the back of my head with force. At first, I didn't turn around. I thought Chris had been shot in the face. I shut my eyes and waited for my own execution. Then I felt the car head reverse and turned just enough to see Chris's hand on the gearshift. As he floored his red hatchback, a shot was fired. Then another. For several blocks we drove backward, refusing to turn around until we were safely out of pistol range. We then drove for several miles in complete silence, too scared to talk about what happened or even stop to brush the glass out of our laps and from our hair.

A couple of weeks later though, I was back to that same corner.

I eventually discovered that buying drugs from shifty characters wasn't the real adventure I craved, though it took me nearly a decade to figure it out. But when I finally gave up drinking and narcotics, I still needed something to fill the adrenaline void, an activity rife with uncertainty and the potential for harm. For a while, I thought I had found it in surfing. The power of big waves and the ocean's indifference to whether I caught its swell or was buried beneath a mountain of roiling white water became my obsession. But surfing's thrills proved insufficient. I tried climbing mountains in Bolivia. Still, I wasn't satisfied. Nothing seemed to come close to the rush of potential violence and self-destruction. And so I became depressed.

Then, on a whim, I went to Haiti during the violent coup and inadvertently found what would fill the void nicely. I wanted to understand the compulsions that prompted someone to kill and butcher their victims like those I saw in Haiti. I thought it was a noble endeavor that could satiate my own addictions and serve a purpose.

A year later, I went to Afghanistan and Iraq for the first time, then went back again and again. I was hooked and constantly looking for ways to up the ante. What used to frighten me soon became mundane. When I had to cover domestic stories to make the rent, I was suffocating in my own mediocrity and boredom, more depressed than ever. In Miami, I distracted myself from my doldrums with a new love, one that initially felt genuine and capable of curing me of my self-destructive habits. I would have to be better, for her.

But it didn't work. I eventually grew to resent the attention that our problems were taking from my ambitions, which is why I ran back to Afghanistan last year while our relationship was falling apart.

In the weeks following my injury, I thought my addiction was cured. But the compulsion toward risk came back, prompting me to take senseless chances even while I was recovering. I think I did it because I worried I might never be back here, never find myself at the vortex of situations out of my control. When I thought I might never work again, I felt like I had no reason to live. I sunk deeper than I'd ever gone. I began thinking of ways out. When I wasn't racing Miami's highways helmetless at night, I would sometimes ride past a gun store on Route 41, just west of the city on the way to the Everglades. A few times I stopped in the parking lot and just sat there. I figured Florida was one of those states with fast-and-loose gun laws that would allow me to buy something compact and powerful in the alley behind the store without a wait or registration. From there I'd keep heading west until the cell reception dropped, about a third of the way between Miami and Naples. Then I'd take one of the dirt roads that bisects vast expanses of reeds and waist-high waters. There I could finally end it. No one would hear the shot. The Everglades' predators would take care of the rest.

I think about this while staring at the bed in which two strangers are sharing a sandwich. That bed is a milepost on a destructive path that nearly ended my life not once, but twice.

I convinced myself coming back here would save me.


I am fully cognizant of how unhealthy all this is and that being back in Afghanistan is feeding my destructive tendencies. Opposing forces pull at me all the time—the ability to recognize my problem and a penchant for ignoring that recognition. What really scares me, more than getting my legs blown off or getting shot again, is that one day the wrong side of this struggle is going to win and I won't be able to talk myself back toward the rationale for living. I'll just keep pushing, either here or another conflict, or someplace else, doing something ill-advised and stupid, hoping that it eventually results in my demise.

My greatest fear is me.

*Can't fixate on this now. I have too much to do.*

I take a last look at my bed and bid its new inhabitants goodbye, then head back to my room to finish writing the eye injury story.

# CHAPTER 31
# THE LUCKIEST FUCK

JUNE 15, 2011
FORWARD OPERATING BASE FENTY, NANGARHAR PROVINCE, AFGHANISTAN

Fenty is a major hub for NATO operations in eastern Afghanistan. It's on the outskirts of Jalalabad, the country's third largest city, and located on what used to be a civilian airport. It's said Osama bin Laden landed here when he first arrived in Afghanistan, after he was unceremoniously given the boot from Sudan. Considering the decade of war resulting from harboring the al Qaida leader, I'm guessing the Taliban probably wishes they could take a mulligan on that decision and instead redirect his plane to nearby Peshawar. Would have saved them a lot of headaches, considering he wound up in Pakistan anyway.

*Woulda, coulda, shoulda...*

Many drone missions bound for Pakistan are flown out of Fenty. The drones occasionally emerge during the day from a super-secret hangar on the other side of the flightline. Mostly they operate at night, a lesson I learned the hard way. One time I didn't feel like waiting for a runway crosswalk to turn green, so I bolted blindly across the tarmac in the dark. About halfway to the other side, I heard something approach in the blackness that sounded like an enormous electric weedwacker. I sprinted the last few strides just as the wingtip of a Predator drone—its whirling propellers capable of mincing me into confetti—rolled passed me.

Despite my near shredding, Fenty is my favorite base in Afghanistan. Also known as "Jbad," it has a frontier town feel about it, without the rampant gambling, gunfights, or prostitution (that I know of). Sure, there's plenty of brass and rules here, but not nearly as many as Bagram, where military police prowl the roads trying to catch anyone going faster than the posted 10 miles per hour, issuing tickets to offenders.

But just like Tombstone or Dodge City, Fenty is a center for commerce. Out here the bootleg movies are plentiful at the "Hajji Shops," the admittedly less-than-politically-correct name given the small stores on base owned by Afghan locals. But that's what everyone calls these small plywood storefronts where you can buy the latest movies, T-shirts letting everyone know you're an Afghan Commando, butterfly knives, and jewelry of dubious origin.

I'm cooling my heels here until I can get to my next embed in Kunar, the province where I was injured. I'm not heading back to Pirtle King—I don't think I'm mentally prepared for that—but my embed is with a unit not far from PK that sees plenty of action.

While waiting to grab a free seat on a helicopter, I spend my days hanging out in the office of military public affairs, where Major David Eastburn is in charge.

Eastburn is about my age. I quickly come to learn we share a similar Midwestern sensibility predicated on our mutual refusal to suffer fools and stuffed shirts. How he's managed to hold his tongue while dealing with Army brass during his long, eventful career is an impressive display of self-discipline. Maybe it's because he served in Iraq alongside the Marines in Fallujah, the scene of some of the worst fighting in that war. Having dealt with his share of overbearing commanders, putting up with reporter ding-dongs like me causes him few headaches in comparison, though some days I'm certain he'd rather be tussling with al Qaida than juggling whiny journalists asking the military to cater to their every need.

He's a straight shooter, a rarity among public affairs, some of whom like to sugarcoat the shit. It took me a couple of days to figure this out about him. In hindsight, I probably should have discerned it the moment he introduced himself.

"So when I heard we were getting the shot-in-the-face guy, I had to look you up," he says when introducing himself.

"Yep," is all I reply in wary response. Since I've been back in Afghanistan, I'm not always certain how much I should reveal about my previous misadventure here. I've retold the story a handful of times and typically get one of two reactions. Mostly it's mouth-agape, head-shaking astonishment and assertions they'd never heard anything like that.

A few times I got the feeling those I told consider me an undeservingly lucky prick, that my fortune is perhaps unfair to those that weren't so blessed, friends and fellow combatants who went home with fewer body parts, or worse, in a casket. I get that, which is why I've become hesitant about discussing it in details unless asked.

Eastburn lets me know in which camp he resides when he introduces himself.

"I saw that video of you getting shot. You are by far the luckiest fuck I ever met," he says laughing.


In some ways, Eastern and his public affairs team do a job similar to mine. They also go out to combat outposts, interview soldiers, and tell their stories for in-house, American military media. However, I've seen some of the footage of firefights they get and it blows mine away.

The other difference is their work is not unbiased. But then again, neither is mine. As much as I try to be objective, I admittedly push harder while questioning higher-ups and occasionally ease off on the men and women at the front, justifying my slack due to their continued hardships and constant threat of death. I try to correct course when writing my stories, keeping in mind the old George Orwell credo about how "journalism is printing what someone else does not want printed: everything else is public relations."

But living up to the letter of Orwell's assertion is difficult in Afghanistan, especially since I'm only covering the war from one side. The Taliban doesn't have an official embed program unless you count kidnapping. A handful of reporters have gotten in with them, covered the fighting from their side and come back with incredible stories. Alas, I am not one of them.

As it is, I couldn't do my job without military public affairs and as such I make it a point to get along with them as best I can. Without them arranging for me to get seats on flights out to the combat outposts, I'd never get anywhere.

I've had a few run-ins with a handful of Public Affairs Officers over the years, but mostly it's been smooth going. I have a "tread lighter, get further" attitude when working with them so I don't come off like an entitled reporter prick.

Eastburn's public affairs staff comprises Staff Sgt. Amber Robinson, who goes by "Sgt. Rob," a lanky, brassy blonde with short-cropped hair and a boyfriend back in Hawaii that looks exactly like the Cobra Kai bad guy Johnny in *Karate Kid*. When they talk on Skype, which is often, I try to come up with new ways to crack wise about his resemblance. I refresh my memory on the movie's IMDB page to get my zingers down pat.

"Fear does not exist in this dojo, does it?" I yell across the room when Sgt. Rob is trying to enjoy a not-so-private moment with her beau.

"We do not train to be merciful here! Mercy is for the weak!"

My hokey pop-culture references are mercifully lost on Khyber Hotak, an Afghan translator and facilitator for Fenty public affairs. Units come and go, but Khyber is always here, risking his neck to work with the Americans. The Taliban targets those who help the foreign forces, yet he's been doing it for years.

Then there's Sgt. Ginifer Spada, who's planning her nuptials to her fiancé back in Alabama while covering the war and sounds an awful lot like Napoleon Dynamite when expressing both genuine and feigned exasperation. "Gaaawd!"

Sgt. Ewlyn Lovelace asks me about his job prospects in journalism were he to leave the military. I don't have the heart to tell him he'd be better off aspiring to a career pulling peanuts out of elephant shit than hoping for a lucrative career as a reporter. Out on assignment is photographer Staff Sgt. Mark Burrell, who I'm told bears an uncanny resemblance to John McEnroe and apparently hates when people point it out. I sit at his desk when I'm in their office whiling away the time till a spot opens up for me on a helicopter heading to Kunar.

Tucked in the opposite corner on the other side the room is another female soldier whose name I never catch, though later learn is referred as the "The Treasure Troll." She's named as such for her shock of red hair and stout physique reminiscent of one of those eraser adornments children place on their pencils.

The Treasure Troll is busy telling no one in particular, but loud enough for the entire room to hear, about how she and her boyfriend back home like to engage in rough sex acts and bondage fantasies that include whip play and hot candle wax dripping into orifices I'd rather not envision. Her graphic disclosures of intimate moments permeate the room with skin-crawling discomfort and dangles awkwardly like an off-color joke told to the wrong crowd.

The only person in the room not visibly unnerved by the repugnant retelling of foreign objects crammed into her and her boyfriend's body cavities is the man sitting across from her, Tom Peter, a reporter for the *Christian Science Monitor*. Tom is listening to this nauseating tale of erotica gone wrong with a pensive expression and no apparent discomfort. I sort of know Tom. We met once last year at Bagram and spoke briefly before being shuttled off on our respective embeds, mine being at Pirtle King. But that wasn't the last time I saw him. While returning late at night from my recent embed in Kandahar, I found Tom curled up on the floor in a narrow, dusty hallway outside the rooms where reporters sleep at Bagram. Apparently all the rooms were locked, so he plopped down right on the wooden floor, using a rolled-up foam sleeping pad for a pillow. I remember thinking he looked like a Depression-era hobo, catching a few winks on the floor of a boxcar.

What little I think I know of Tom comes mainly from my observations of him that night. Like me, he seems at ease with certain kinds of discomfort, like sleeping wherever necessary. However, he's obviously more tolerant of strangers discussing their sexual proclivities. Not once does he look away from The Treasure Troll during her wistful recollections of leather-clad erotica. Instead, he is seemingly enraptured by her story, as if listening to an exquisitely performed piano concerto.

I too begin to enjoy it. Not so much the story—that's still gross—but the company. I've missed this. This is where I belong: neck-deep in the abhorrent details of ugly-people lust and Tom's apparent ease with it. During the early days of my recovery, there were always people around, yet I was lonely. My loneliness was further exacerbated by my double-dealing with Tatiana and Fernanda, a final kick in the urethra by my ex, and my subsequent, self-imposed exile to The Failure Cave. But now that I'm back in Afghanistan and among my kind, I feel a kinship that only comes from spending time in places like this, where everyone is a stranger in a strange land trying to make do, ward off their respective loneliness, and eventually go home in one piece. These are my people. And I am theirs. Tom and I are from the same strain of misfit toys of journalism. Eastern and the others in the Public Affairs office seem like good folk to me and I like them, which is unusual because I don't come by friends easily.

When The Treasure Troll finishes her story, no one utters a word for a long beat. Then Tom chimes in.

"Hmmm, that's incredible. It reminds me of something that happened to me just recently," he says, proceeding to tell a story of sexual dysfunction so abhorrent and disquieting that even I am shocked and speechless.

# CHAPTER 32
# BRUINS WIN AND MORTARS RAIN

JUNE 16, 2011
COMBAT OUTPOST HONAKER MIRACLE, KUNAR PROVINCE, AFGHANISTAN

Sgt. Lawrence Teza is in his barracks when an explosion rips the hinges off the building's steel door, spraying his left side with shrapnel and breaking his hand.

"When the bombing started I was counting all my men . . . then *wham!*" Teza says later with a faint smile while recounting the attack. His torso is pock marked with numerous open wounds and his hand is set in a cast.

I'm decidedly luckier than Teza at the onset of the attack. While he's accounting for the soldiers in his squad and sustaining injuries, I'm outside on my way to the showers. When the first mortar hits, I run back to the barracks for cover, a scramble that proves painstakingly difficult in my flip-flops. There I hunker down with a group of soldiers in their quarters. There's little else to do during a mortar attack other than find shelter and wait for the barrage to end. Sometimes it's only a few minutes. But this is a long one. The *tat-tat-tat* of small-arms fire and booming sounds of mortars last for hours. I've waited out my share of Taliban attacks, but seeing as I'm still getting my nerve back, this one has me sufficiently spooked. I'm trying my best to not to show it while shooting the shit with the guys and watching bootleg DVDs of the latest super-hero offering of the summer. Fortunately, the one we're watching proves an ideal distraction. It's so terrible it's gone from "bad," to schlocky sci-fi "good-bad," all the way back to "bad" again.

*My lord,* Green Lantern *is a train wreck. I'd almost rather step outside and take my chances getting blown up than watch Ryan Reynolds prance around in a CGI dayglow-green leotard.*

I was just beginning to feel a little better about being back, in that during the last couple of weeks I haven't had one major freak-out. Granted, I've been working in the relatively safe confines of larger bases. Still, the fear that swelled in me during the Celine Dion incident back in Ghundy Ghar had retracted and I figured myself cured of my fear. Until the attack here. Either that, or the tremors I'm trying to hide while watching *Green Lantern* are a first sign of an undiagnosed neurological disorder that will kill me if the Taliban doesn't do it first.

I should have known this would happen. Mortar attacks are pretty common here. Since their unit deployed in April, about 10 percent of the company at Honaker Miracle has been injured in blasts. None killed, which is extremely fortunate considering the damage a single round can do. One mortar recently landed inside the wire and set ablaze a multi-ton truck used for towing disabled armored vehicles. The charred wreckage is still sitting in the motor pool.

Now that it's June, the fighting season is in full swing and there's been an uptick in harassing gunfire and IEDs planted in the roads around the combat outpost. Taliban are emboldened by the fact that there are fewer American troops here in the Pech River Valley than in years past. The last time I was here a couple years ago, Combat Outpost Honaker Miracle was just one of four bases in this valley. These days it's the lone American-occupied base. Two others have been turned over to the Afghans. The fourth, COP Michigan, was closed and razed. I did an embed there a couple of years ago. Such a nasty place. They took small arms and mortar fire all the time. Day and night. It was such a magnet for Taliban attacks that Michigan gained notoriety in the civilian world back home. A men's magazine dubbed the space where Michigan soldiers worked out as the "most dangerous gym in the world" because its walls were riddled with bullet holes from the frequent attacks it sustained.

Now that I'm just down the road from where it stood my impulse for self-preservation is telling me to keep my venturing to a minimum, running contradictory to the apparent false sense of confidence I'd experienced just a couple days before when I tagged along on a foot patrol just a short stroll up a hill from Honaker Miracle.

We're on an early-morning foot patrol to a nearby village. Leaving the trucks back at Honaker Miracle, the platoon heads out of the gate and walks in the quiet dawn along a dry creek bed that leads to a narrow dirt path snaking up a hillside to a small group of homes. A lieutenant stops to talk to the locals, asking if they've seen any Taliban lately. The guys scan the slopes leading up the mountain for any potential gunmen.

Then, there's a murmur among the soldiers. They start talking about getting out of there, and fast.

"Sir, this is bigger than you!" one of them says with desperation in his voice. "This is bigger than all of us!"

The lieutenant acquiesces. We leave the village, hustle down the hillside and back to the outpost with the kind of urgency usually reserved for responses to enemy fire.

After throwing down their kit, some of the soldiers gather around a TV in their small mess hall. The picture is fuzzy, the audio garbled. They strain in silence to make out the action. There's a roaring sound coming from the TV. The guys watching rush outside, screaming, waving their arms. A voice comes over the loudspeaker: "The Boston Bruins have just won the Stanley Cup!" The soldier's voice echoes across the river valley and through the nearby mountains where the Taliban are preparing to lob mortars on them in the coming days, injuring Sgt. Teza and scaring the wits out of me.

# CHAPTER 33
# WHORING ON THE FOURTH

JULY 4, 2011
BAGRAM AIRFIELD, PARWAN PROVINCE, AFGHANISTAN

The July sun glinting off Senator John McCain's naked scalp as he strolls across the tarmac is both blinding and worrisome.

*Hasn't this guy had skin cancer like a half dozen times? I can't believe his wife would let him go to Afghanistan without a hat. I bet she gives him an earful when he gets home.*

The senator from Arizona is flanked by his fellow Capitol Hill mates, Senators Joe Lieberman and Lindsey Graham. The trio from the Senate Armed Services Committee are in Afghanistan because it's the Fourth of July, and spending a patriotic holiday in a war zone is political gold. They just landed at Bagram, where I also happen to be following my last embed, a stint with a unit in Nangarhar Province that was relatively uneventful compared to my time at Honaker Miracle. I spent a few days tagging along on patrols through villages close enough to the Pakistani border that many of the shops and residents use rupees instead of Afghanistan's currency, the Afghani. The Taliban were laying IEDs in the roads, attacking a police station, and harassing locals at night. None of that happened while I was there, fortunately. It used to be that I'd get pissed if I didn't get caught in at least one firefight. Now I thank my lucky stars for a "boring embed." I'm guessing those guys have a long summer ahead of them.

America's birthday has drawn all the big guns to Bagram, including General Petraeus, who's on his way out as commander of all NATO forces in Afghanistan. He's getting high marks in Washington for stepping into the fray following the Gen. McChrystal clusterfuck.

No chance I'll ever get that kind of candor from Petraeus, especially considering my disastrous interview with him last month. The guy watches every "p" and "q." It's rumored he has political aspirations—maybe even presidential ones. We probably won't know till after the book the woman from that briefing is writing comes out. That's when you make your move in DC. Until then, he's got his fancy new gig as CIA director.

I wade through a throng of the general's military and civilian sycophants to ask him a question for my token "Fourth of July in Afghanistan" story. I ask Petraeus about the recent uptick in violence now that we're a couple months into fighting season and he gives me the same flavorless spiel from our last interview about "fragile and reversible" gains.

*This guy is a machine. He'll be a player, no doubt.*

I decide I'll lead my story with the wholly uninspiring and insipid Petraeus comments then tack on whatever the senators say with some color about celebrating Independence Day amid a war. Holiday stories from here can come off a little puffy and overtly patriotic. I'll need to be careful I don't let the day's pomp and ceremony whitewash the truth about what's happening here.

The senators aren't here for the hotdogs and Bagram 5K run. All three are irked by President Obama's recent announcement that he plans to draw down a third of the 100,000 American troops currently in the country by September 2012.

McCain says it's too many, too soon. Eastern Afghanistan is still up for grabs. Other parts of the country are firmly in Taliban control. I'm not sure which way I lean on the proposed drawdown. The Afghan forces aren't ready to secure this country by themselves. But they likely never will be. It's been ten years. Maybe enough is enough. Time for America and NATO allies to wrap this up and cross their fingers. Then again, this place could easily slip into civil war if the US pulls out too quickly. It's a tough call.

Fortunately for me, I don't have to decide, though I do have to stare at a troublesome-looking mole on McCain's forehead while he tells me what he thinks.

"We try to remind our fellow citizens that the attack of 9/11 began here in Afghanistan," McCain tells me, hitting his target audience in the Venn Diagram sweet spot of patriotism and fear of future terror attacks. "And it's not in our national security interest to see Afghanistan return to a base for attacks on the United States of America and our allies."

I decide that since I have all three of them lined and up and raring to fire off their best anti-drawdown rhetoric, I'm going to rate them best to worst.

*Not bad, McCain. You're currently the leader, though only by default because you went first.*

I personally like the guy, though don't always agree with his politics. Plus, he is a war hero that endured years of torture and capture. He's the real deal. That said, he needs some sunblock, ASAP.

*Next up is Droopy Dog, err, Lieberman.*

The Connecticut lawmaker looks like he hasn't slept since his failed bid for the vice presidency in 2000.

*Someone get the guy a fistful of Ambien and the number for Senator John Kerry's plastic surgeon.*

"Our disagreement with the president was about the pace of the withdrawal, how quickly," Lieberman drones in a monotone that could soothe the most savage and rabid of beasts. "Because we think that all of them, or most of them, should stay here through this fighting season and next fighting season, through October."

*Not doing it. I'm already calling it: you're last, Lieberman, unless your buddy Lindsey completely shits the bed.*

Graham gets into it slowly at first, going folksy with his assertions that all the troops should stay.

*Is he being folksy? Sometimes I can't tell with Southerners. To me, the South Carolina senator sounds like someone who hangs out behind his barn, sipping sour mash while spinning yarns riddled with down-home wisdom.*

The Afghan people "do not want to go back to the Taliban way of life," he starts off his response to my question about the drawdown. He's setting himself up for a theatrical finish, a money-shot quote. I can feel it. "That means that the people of Afghanistan can maintain their freedom and what happened here," he says, turning toward the memorial at Bagram commemorating the September 11 attacks, "never happens again."

The senator just needs to snap off his point with the right metaphor coupled with a fairy-tale scenario for a happy ending to American involvement in Afghanistan.

"My goal is that when we leave one day, that we will have an enduring relationship as far as the eye can see, and we never have to come back to this country except as guests."

*Ding! Ding! Ding! There you have it folks! Graham is the winner!*

He hit the spike square on the head with the patriot's carnival mallet, ringing the bell that declares him the champion Republican patriot of the bunch.

*He's a charming son of a bitch, I'll give him that.*

# CHAPTER 34
# DIRT COOKIES

JULY 12, 2011
KABUL, AFGHANISTAN

My Afghanistan cell phone buzzes just after 8 a.m. Its rumbling reverberates through the particleboard nightstand like the low-grade guitar amp of a Kinks cover band.

I'm already awake, though not fully conscious, just lounging in bed, thinking about breakfast and the story I have to file. Returned to my Kabul guesthouse yesterday after another embed. I've got a few more lined up with the Army and Marines and a couple stories in Kabul I'm trying to flesh out. I've decided to stay here at least through the summer, possibly longer, if *USA Today* will keep paying me.

I have enough work to keep myself busy this morning. Cameras, notebooks, and a tangle of cables are in a pile on the desk next to my computer. I purposefully put them there last night to guilt myself into tackling it first thing. I'll get to it after a not-so-hearty meal of undercooked eggs, stale bread, half a dozen cups of green tea, and three cigarettes—my morning ritual at the Diana.

The buzzing persists.

*Let's see who the hell this is . . .*

Caller ID says it's a radio editor in New York.

*Blegh . . . What do they want?*

Must be around midnight there. I'm annoyed at the intrusion into my all-too-brief-twilight nirvana.

I answer and a voice starts without the formality of a hello.

"Can you file on the Karzai killing?"

I groggily agree, having no idea what the editor half a world away is talking about.

"I'm on it," I assure him. "I was just following that up with some sources," I say in a harried tone, feigning industriousness.

*He has to know I'm clueless.*

My warbling voice is the product of sheer panic at the idea that the president of Afghanistan was assassinated and I, like a dolt, slept right through it.

I turn on my computer. Beads of sweat run down my brow while it boots up at a leisurely pace due to its age and frequent visits to certain cookie-laden websites offering erotica. I bounce my knee and bite the nail on my right index finger, waiting for it to finish.

*Come on. Come on. Get online, you fucker.*

The connection at my guesthouse is painfully slow. Good thing the generator is running. Kabul's power grid is often overloaded and brownouts are frequent. Sometimes I have to implore the staff to turn it on when I need the Internet. This is how a one-man reporting band in Afghanistan operates.

*Here we go. Open browser. Google. Google News. Headlines.*

First one:

"Afghan president's half brother killed"

*Whew!*

Dodged a bullet there. I mean me, not him.

"Him" is Ahmed Wali Karzai, who was shot at close range by a visitor who smuggled a weapon into a meeting. So much for comprehensive pat downs.

This sort of thing happens all the time in Afghanistan. Ministers and other lawmakers are regular targets for shooters and suicide bombers. When it's someone of relative importance here it will warrant space in most print outlets, though not cable news. They're usually too busy stalking Casey Anthony and other tabloid detritus.

But when the president of Afghanistan's half brother gets killed, everyone shows interest, enough to remind editors and the American public, albeit only temporarily, that yes, there is a war still being fought in Afghanistan, and yes, more than 100,000 American soldiers are doing the fighting and dying over here, not to mention hundreds of thousands of Afghans in uniform and NATO troops from around the world. They're up against the Taliban and other hardline militants lurking in the mountains and shadows of every town and city. It's a full-on, throw-down war, the longest in which America has ever been involved, not that anyone is paying attention, except when a big story like this breaks.

I scan the wire services for their take on the news, make a couple of phone calls to confirm what I've already read, then bang out a short brief and email it to the news desk in New York. I read it over a few times, make a correction, and then ready my radio persona, a phony, rusty-throat baritone devoid of accent with just the right emphasis on certain syllables to grab the attention of rush-hour zombies stuck in gridlock, crawling to jobs they can't stand.

**Afghan security officials say the half brother of the country's president was killed by a gunman.**

**They say Ahmed Wali Karzai was shot in the head and chest by a member of his inner circle before his bodyguards killed his assailant.**

**No one is claiming responsibility for the assassination, though some say they suspect the Taliban.**

**The president's brother was a powerbroker in Afghanistan's Kandahar Province, the birthplace of the Taliban.**

**He allegedly had ties to both the opium trade and US government intelligence agencies.**

**Carmen Gentile, ABC News, Kabul**

I put extra oomph on the "killed" and "shot" for dramatic effect. A little pageantry is essential if you want people to really listen. Make sure I annunciate my name too. It's a little showy, I know. But that's the game.

As more additional details about the killing pour in, I file more spots, making fifty bucks a hit. That's good extra scratch on top of my *USA Today* money. By midmorning I've made a few hundred bucks, more than I make in an entire day spent with US soldiers walking IED-laden footpaths. I contemplate this cruel injustice and remind myself that those same soldiers walk those trails every day, many of whom have seen a buddy have a leg or two blown off on those paths, and get paid much, much less.

Requests from other outlets start rolling in.

"Can you do an on-air appearance on Skype for this TV outlet or a phone call for that radio program?"

I say yes to them all and start keeping a running tab of what I'm owed after each submission. I basically repeat the same thing over and over again. Between hits I see if there are any new developments. Not much has changed. Gunmen killed by the slain Karzai's bodyguards. No one is certain who is responsible. Could be the Taliban. Might be a personal beef.

For reasons I can't quite understand, this story seems to have legs. I can never tell what story is going to resonate with an audience when I'm over here.

*Don't question it, moron. You're making money hand over fist to repeat the same thing over and over again.*

Good thing, too. I'm literally down to a few hundred bucks in the bank. Everything I've made over the last couple of months in Afghanistan has gone to pay off debts incurred during my recovery from last year's injury.

My first month here paid off sailboating in Australia and my assorted adventures in New Zealand. This month is going toward older debts. If interest in this thing keeps up I just might finally pay off that cursed engagement ring. So far today, I've made over a grand and the American East Coast hasn't even woken up yet.


My exuberance at landing a single-day score like this aside—and the admittedly grim glee I feel considering someone did die—my financial windfall is a troubling indicator of the present state of journalism. Few outlets keep a full-time correspondent in Afghanistan, preferring to send people in once in a while to report an easily digestible, state-of-the-war story for the most casual of news consumers. Besides waning interest at home, some editors are reluctant to keep people here anymore because Kabul can be expensive. Wartime economies like Afghanistan's are based on Western dollars and demands, which is why the most expensive hotels in town can cost as much or more than four-star accommodations in Manhattan. Sending a tenderfoot staff reporter to

Afghanistan who isn't willing to scrimp, save, and stay in modest guesthouses can drain an outlet's travel budget by five figures or more, depending on the length of their stay and the stories they do. Want to travel outside the capital by car? Better figure on at least $500 a day in fixer/translator and driver expenses. Most editors won't lay out that kind of money unless you can guarantee you'll come back with Mullah Omar tied up in the trunk and confessing to wearing ladies' underwear.

Even fewer journalists are embedding with the military. I used to meet a half dozen reporters or more while waiting at the larger bases for transportation to my embeds at combat outposts on the front lines of the war. These days, I often have the journalists' quarters all to myself for a day or so till I cross paths with someone else. Here in Kabul, where there used to be hundreds of Western hacks, now only a few dozen remain.

So, not wanting to completely give up on at least pretending to give a shit, some outlets reach out to any available journalist when news breaks to get something, anything, reported in their name. I work with an organization that supplies faces and voices to outlets in situations like these. They are essentially my pimp—they provide the client, and I deliver the goods and give them a cut of my earnings.

TV news needs a visual for the Karzai story, someone to go on the air and talk about what's happening. Ideally the reporter is positioned overlooking something vaguely "Afghanistany" in the background—a mountain, some dusty buildings. That scene, and a warm body wearing something khaki, is all that's really needed to complete the faux tableau of what passes for journalism these days. The smoke-and-mirror aspect of it all would be unbearably nauseating if I weren't making a butt load of dough today while partaking in its sins.

I do a handful of appearances for outlets via Skype from my hotel room with the street outside as my backdrop. Then I get a call from CNN in Atlanta. They need someone to go on the air in a half hour. I agree to do it for 350 bucks and head over to their bureau, just down the street from the Diana. I walk the pockmarked and rutted dirt road and knock on their inch-thick metal security door. The slat opens and I state my purpose for pounding on their fortress gate. The armed guards debate among themselves before allowing me to enter. Their compound, a former private home turned news bureau, is palatial, just like the other news bureaus next door. I head up to their live position with their cameraman and take in the view of the aforementioned mountains and dusty buildings. It's a wooden box with three sides, same as the neighbors' on either side. Apparently, there's very little incentive for originality.

The cameraman readies me by pinning a microphone to my T-shirt. I forgot to wear a collared button-down.

*Oops.*

Then I put in the earpiece to hear the producers and see myself on the monitor as they do in Atlanta. I hear tittering among them and can guess what has them in a tizzy. My two-month-old beard in all its unruly glory is not exactly in line with the polished look of CNN's on-air mannequins: a lock of hair across the forehead and an indigenous scarf thrown over the shoulder is the furthest extent of acceptable dishevelment for the cable news image minders.

"Ummm, we're having problems with the feed, so we're just going do this on the phone," says the voice in my earpiece. I laugh and stick out my tongue for the camera, knowing damn well they can see me. I rattle off the same facts for them that I have a dozen times already today.


This is how the TV news sausage is made. I've done it a lot in recent years, producing numerous stories for cable and network news that paid big money compared with the compensation I get for print work. But I always feel dirty, like I'm cheating on my true love, writing, with a dirty TV whore in the champagne room.

A few years ago I had a TV experience so disheartening it nearly drove me from the business.

I had signed on with Fox News to produce a story about a food shortage in Haiti. The reporter, cameraman, and I flew into Port-au-Prince, where rioting over shortages had left several people dead. I suggested we show just how dire the situation had become by interviewing those that had been most adversely affected by the shortages, residents in the city's slums. Instead, the reporter got it in his head that we should do a piece on "dirt cookies." Some poor Haitians mix butter and salt with mud and eat it to stave off hunger. While certainly a curious tidbit to the larger story of starvation, the reporter wanted it to be a focal point of the piece by actually eating a dirt cookie on camera, which he did. The editors in New York applauded his moxie, while I hung my head in shame.

Hoping to salvage the rest of the assignment, I suggested we get out of the city to see how Haiti's rural poor were faring. The reporter said I should keep my hired-hand ideas to myself and stay out of the way while he and the cameraman did live shots from the balcony of our lovely hotel overlooking the city squalor. I spent the next two days in my room watching reruns of *Diff'rent Strokes* on satellite TV. I did, however, see one of the best episodes of all time, the one where Gordon Jump molests Dudley in the back of his bicycle shop. I called a friend in the states to tell him I caught it. It was almost magical.

So I guess the trip wasn't a total wash.


The Karzai killing dominates the headlines for the rest of the day. After leaving CNN, I head back to the Diana and resume cranking out spots for ABC along with phone and Skype interviews. News desks in London and Paris and outlets in the US ask me the same ridiculous questions over and over again.

"What does this mean for the future of Afghanistan?"

I reply with a rambling, barely coherent explanation about Karzai's many enemies and throw in some historical context about Kandahar being the birthplace of the Taliban, blah, blah, blah. I do this so many times my answers have developed a patter that allows me to rattle off the same nonsense without actually thinking about what I'm saying, not unlike the politicians and generals I sometimes harass for sound bites.

The phone interviews I do with my feet up on my desk while looking at last night's baseball scores. I did a couple outside so I could smoke a cigarette and give my audio some gritty authenticity, until the ice cream man pushed his cart past the Diana playing a twinkly electronic melody. That doesn't sound very "war zoney," so I ducked inside mid-interview.

By nightfall in Kabul the story has a full head of steam. I've been at it for 10 hours and still the requests keep coming.

Hoarse from a full day of nonstop talking, I perform a quick mental tally of the hits I did and estimate I made about $5,000 from the death of Ahmed Wali Karzai. That just about covers what I paid for that engagement ring, minus the taxes.

I'd feel really dirty about what I did today if I could afford to keep my conscience clean.

# CHAPTER 35
# EMBRACE THE SUCK

JULY 23, 2011
OUTPOST 22, UPPER GERESHK VALLEY, HELMAND PROVINCE,
AFGHANISTAN

Marine Sgt. David Sowell smokes a cigarette at a tiny compound in Taliban territory and ponders the possibility of losing a limb in an IED blast.

"I don't want to lose my legs, but if I do, I can cope with it . . . as long as it's not one or both of my arms, I'll be fine," says Sowell in his Texas drawl.

His apparent ease with possible amputation is unnerving considering how earlier today we walked the same footpaths where many of his fellow Marines lost arms and legs. One even went home a triple amputee.

I've been spending the last few days with Sowell and his fellow Marines in the Upper Gereshk Valley. It's just down the way from Sangin, the epicenter of the Helmand Province shit storm that's been raging all summer. Helmand's where the Taliban sends some of its very best, its varsity squad. The fighting has been fierce. When Sowell and his unit arrived a few months ago, they had to claw their way into the valley one firefight at a time. About 50 guys were sent home wounded, many missing at least one limb. Four were killed.

They were dropped in here last spring as part of the US strategy to keep the Taliban on the outskirts while the cities and villages behind the Marines gradually accept the government's help, and in return, pledge their allegiance. At least that's the plan anyway.

Now in midsummer, they have a tenuous foothold in the region and a new home, a compound called "Patrol Base Shark's Tooth." It's a large base by patrol base standards, but its amenities are almost nonexistent. Comprised of mud walls and windowless hovels partially burrowed in the ground, it bears an uncanny resemblance to Luke Skywalker's home on Tatooine.

The Marines live four or more to the tiny, subterranean rooms, providing some relief from the scorching summer sun. But a shortage of housing at Shark's Tooth means some of the younger guys sleep al fresco. Camo netting hung overhead provides a little shade during the day, while insect nets draped over their bunks keep some of the mosquitoes at bay.

There's no running water, of course; the Marines at Shark's Tooth go weeks, even months, without showers. No water also means no latrines or portable toilets, the use of which was made doubly impossible due to the fact that the last two Afghans they'd paid to carry away their feces via "shit trucks"—vehicles with rear-mounted tanks and vacuums for sucking feces out of latrines—were blown up by the Taliban.

In lieu of even rudimentary waste management, they use "wag bags," plastic sacks into which they defecate. After completing their business, they throw their wag bags on the burn pile along with all the other refuse that's incinerated on Shark Tooth's detritus pyre burning around the clock. Noxious gases inside the bags expand in the heat, so when a flame licks one of these engorged receptacles, it emits a loud *pop*, triggering my PTSD until I'm able to differentiate regular shit explosions from live fire.

Despite these terrible conditions, I haven't heard a single Marine gripe about the place. When I do ask one of them to tell me what he misses the most back home, he responds wistfully, "A clean place to take a dump," the way one might mention a forthcoming trip to the Bahamas. The others deride his softness with a chorus of ball busting and assertions that their buddy is a real "pussy."

It's even rougher living at this small satellite compound, where platoons take turns manning the place to keep the Taliban just that much farther away from the main highway, and Shark's Tooth. It's comprised of a nine-foot exterior wall around a handful of rooms and a well with water they can't drink lest they become violently ill, a hard lesson already learned. Once when they ran out of bottled water, the Marines drank from the well out of desperation. Shortly thereafter the entire platoon came down with stomach ailments so severe they were forced to hang their bare asses over the sides of the walls so their rancid waste wouldn't collect around their ankles. This nightmarish event is retold to me with great relish and laughter by several of those who endured the gut-twisting agony.

When we arrive here, a handful of young Marines pile into a windowless room covered with dirty carpets to relax. I enter and ask them what it's like spending the night in a place where they've been attacked in the past and likely will be again. They chuckle, offer a few cracks about squalid conditions and the heat. Most skirt the issue about the dangers faced here. Petty Officer 3rd Class Kurtis Lett, a Navy corpsman attached to the Marines, offers his candid assessment.

"This place isn't really that bad if you're not scared of getting shot at or blown up," he says. The others nod in agreement.

Outside some other Marines are playing cards. One of them produces his iPod and puts on the Rebecca Black song "Friday" in celebration of the week's end, a song whose monotone Auto-Tuned chorus has burrowed into nearly every American's subconscious, much to our collective chagrin.

Amid their banter about which pop star is more bangable, and ball busting over who's the worst Spades player, the talk turns to whether it's better to get your legs or arms blown off. "As long as my dick doesn't get blown off, I can live without my legs," says Sowell, adding to his previous preference of not losing his arms over here. They play cards well into the night before some bed down for a couple of hours of sleep. The rest keep watch for the Taliban lurking in the shadows.

Marines are among the military's best practitioners of an essential wartime survival skill: a dark sense of humor. Having one is essential to the preservation of your sanity. Without it, the constant threat of death and dismemberment would break the even the toughest among them.

When I first started covering wars, I didn't understand this attitude—how some soldiers and Marines could joke about death. I figured their bravado was an act for my benefit. They wanted me to portray them as hardened badasses in my stories. But after my first close call I learned that dark humor helps ease the strain during even the most dangerous situations.

Back in 2005, I was riding in the lead Humvee through the narrow streets of a pro-Saddam town in northern Iraq called Hawijah. In the distance we heard a loud *pop* followed by the whooshing sound I know all too well from when I was shot in the head last year.

"RPG, RPG, twelve o'clock!" Spc. John Alden shouted from behind the wheel as the rocket headed toward the driver's side, before veering off course, hitting the pavement a few feet away, ricocheting off the ground, and exploding. Alden gunned the truck toward some men about 100 yards away who jumped into a four-door sedan and sped off. A chorus of Rebel Yells and gleeful "Whoops!" filled the truck as the seven-and-a-half-ton vehicle sideswiped parked cars that tipped and landed in mangled heaps on cracked axles.

The assailants' vehicle turned a corner and vanished from sight. When our truck arrived moments later, their car was abandoned. All four doors were open, its occupants nowhere to be found. Sniper fire rang out, peppering the vehicles, while Blackhawks circled overhead.

Disappointed they'd lost their attackers, the soldiers' spirits were buoyed however by what they found inside the car. In addition to a sniper rifle, the RPG launcher and Iraqi ID cards, the attackers left behind a video camera. Back at their base, the soldiers replayed the tape, gasping and laughing at footage of the attack and the start of their pursuit. They replayed it a half dozen times for others who couldn't believe our fortune and gave them hell for letting the perpetrators slip away.

"We've needed this day for so long," a young lieutenant told me smiling, noting how hard his men had fought against an often-elusive enemy.

Though still shaken by the incident, I then began to understand their exuberance. Skirting a close one calls for a good laugh, if only to keep you from cracking up.

I see that same attitude in the Marines here. They've been on the wrong end of too many Taliban attacks, seen good friends killed, others sent home severely injured, yet they joke around every chance they get. To them, humor is an essential survival skill honed by violence and loss. The more they hurt, the more they need to laugh.

I get that. My own dark sense of humor served me well after I got hurt. It kept me from going stir crazy during my recovery. For a while there I'd lost it, instead wallowing in self-pity over a woman's scorn, taking my hurt out on everyone who cared for me.

But here, among the Marines and soldiers I've spent much of the summer with, I've finally got it back.

Oddly, only in Afghanistan am I able to really laugh again.

# CHAPTER 36
# "BODYGUARDS" REMINDER

AUGUST, 15, 2011
BAGRAM AIRFIELD, AFGHANISTAN

Following a short stint in Kabul to work on a couple of civilian-angle stories, I'm back at Bagram, again. Seems like I'm always coming or going from here. By now I know this place better than the town where I grew up.

After settling in, I check my messages and see I have an email from Ingrid Belqaid. Ingrid is the assistant to my former editor at CBS Radio, Constance Lloyd, the one who met me at the airport in New York nearly a year ago.

The subject line causes cold pricklies to run up my neck.

"Is this your ex?"

*Fuck me.*

My ex hasn't been anywhere near the forefront of my mind these last few months. I've had little time or inclination to dwell on past miseries relating to her. Those caught in the middle of this war have it way worse. Dwelling on my own problems would seem shameful and obnoxious. That's the unfortunate beauty of covering war: your personal problems are a pittance in comparison to those caught in the crossfire.

I leave Ingrid's email unopened for a few hours until curiosity gets the best of me.

*What could it be?*

Perhaps another one of her barbs aimed at discrediting me. My ex sent a number of hateful emails to friends following our breakup, telling them what a horrid piece of shit I am. Haven't heard from her for some time. Perhaps she's just now getting around to fucking up my professional life.

*Maybe it's her wedding announcement.*

I stare at that unopened email, until I screw up the balls to open it.

In the body of Ingrid's message is an article from a women's magazine titled "The Bodyguards." It's a story about female Diplomatic Security agents tasked with protecting Secretary of State Hillary Clinton. The photo accompanying it is of women training in hand-to-hand combat.

*Yep. There she is. My ex is in the picture.*

Ingrid has cut and pasted just the header and quotes from her:

*The Bodyguards*
*To be a woman on the secretary of state's security detail, you have to be fast, smart, and tough . . .*
*Below are my ex's quotes.*
*(name redacted), 37*

**Feminine qualities help. It's the whole mama-bear thing, protecting her cubs. Your whole goal is to take someone down—with a brachial strike, or with a weapon you're firing center mass.**

**I was an attorney before. Shooting and tactical driving were really new to me. In Haiti, at the airport, people were standing there staring in awe. First of all, you're a woman, and second of all, you're holding a gun. Jesse Jackson landed. We were trying to get him to the car. He started peeling off money from his wallet. We were holding people back. Later, I was like, Wow, this is so different from my last job!**

I remember my ex telling me about the melee Jesse caused when he made it rain twenties outside the airport. She and I were tangled up in the sheets of a hotel bed in a Santo Domingo. I had just driven across the border from Haiti with Tatiana and others at the end of my assignment; she was on a break from her duties, heading back to Port-au-Prince in a couple of days. We spent what little time we had together touring the old city and talking about our future, full of hope and excitement.

It was the last good time we had. She returned from Haiti broken by what she had seen. Cried often. Drank even more. That seems like decades ago . . . I finally told her I couldn't be with someone who was always drunk because of my own problems with addiction and alcohol abuse. She stopped for a while, then resumed getting wrecked most nights. She accused me of self-righteousness, a valid point.

I reread the email a dozen times, recalling the darkest days of our relationship and subsequent breakup, memories I'd packed away while I was here, hoping I'd somehow never revisit them.

My first instinct is to reply to Ingrid's email with a well-crafted arsenal of insults aimed at my ex. But there's no point. I'm over her. Any hurt I might be experiencing is a phantom pang from old injuries that have since scarred over.

I snap Ingrid a short reply. "Yes. That's her. But she is not mine anymore."

# CHAPTER 37
# FORTUNATE PEOPLE PROBLEMS
SEPTEMBER 9, 2011
KABUL, AFGHANISTAN

I truly pity the poor sap at the Transportation and Security Administration that will go through my backpack upon its arrival in the states. I stuffed wretched, soiled clothing into the airtight, rubberized receptacle; filthy socks and rancid underwear line the bottom of the bag in neat, deceptive balls of putridness that will fester and ferment in the bellies of two planes before reaching Dulles International a day later.

I'm certain my bag will be scrutinized by security because it always is. Every time I dump its contents after a long assignment, invariably a TSA slip flutters out of the sack and onto the pile of clothes I ought to have burned rather than brought home. Agents might argue doing so constitutes a transportation-of-deadly-chemical-agents infraction.

I haven't had much time to wash anything these last few weeks, is the lie I tell myself to allay my guilt for not at least bucket rinsing my underwear. Instead, I blame the fact that I crammed in as much reporting as I could before my flight back to the States for why my clothes reek.

After my Helmand embed, I returned to Kabul briefly to work on a story about Afghan amputees making their way in a country where there's little institutional assistance for the disabled. I interviewed women with missing legs who managed to not only find work, but thrive in a society that stigmatizes them as largely unsuited for marriage or anything else. "After it happened

I thought I was useless and the rest of my life meaningless," Amina Azimi said, recalling how she lost her leg when an RPG crashed through her home and exploded. Instead of wallowing, Amina picked herself up and found her way into radio, where she hosts a program about the millions of Afghans living with disabilities. It's one of those inspiring stories heavy on sentimentality that occasionally gives me a fleeting glimmer of hope for the future of this country.

Then I went back to Nangarhar on a last-minute invite to a combat outpost near the Pakistani border, where the close quarters shared by US and Afghan forces in an abandoned police station made for interesting living dynamics. Typically, US and Afghan forces live separately due to their "varying" living standards (i.e., Afghan forces are poorly funded, which means they often live worse than some street dogs) and the fear of the "Green on Blue" attacks that have been on the rise in Afghanistan this summer. So far a number of Afghan forces or Taliban posing as soldiers have turned their weapons on NATO soldiers, killing several and wounding many others.

However, a first sergeant at Combat Outpost Sherzad warned me against visiting the Afghan troops in their wing of their shared quarters for a very different reason. "Don't go up there alone," he says gesturing toward the staircase leading to Afghan barracks. "I don't. It smells like butt sex and shame." I later ignore his thinly veiled assertion that I could be sexually molested by their ranks and interview some soldiers living in the still, rank air of the windowless barracks.

My last embed was the "get" of this trip: rarely granted access to an American Green Beret unit living among Afghans at a small base in a village in rural Paktia Province.

The Taliban refer to the Special Forces as the "Bearded Bastards" due to their penchant for growing wooly facial hair. The elite soldiers also forgo traditional uniforms, wearing civilian clothes and speaking Pashtun to locals and heading out on long missions in the mountains to capture and kill "high-value targets": senior Taliban leaders and the like. I didn't get to see anything that sexy during the few days I was with them—just some meetings with local Afghan police, who they train, and a patrol through the village. Still, readers love that elite soldier stuff and my editor at *USA Today* promises me it will make the front page.

A cover would be a first for anything I've ever written from here.

A series of delayed departures due to inclement weather in the mountains during my embed with the Green Berets has me leaving Afghanistan on the one-year anniversary of the day I was shot, a contrived sense of symmetry that resonates with no one but me. To celebrate a successful return without major incident or melodrama, I snap off a smug tweet to the Taliban noting the date and taunting them for not getting me this time around. I momentarily consider that my arrogance transcends standard douchiness and has crossed over into abject stupidity. Not that the Taliban is keeping tabs on me. I'm certain I'm not even on their radar. They have far more pressing matters to which they must attend: recruiting children for suicide bombings, stoning women, shaking down farmers for protection money . . .

Still I immediately regret fucking with them on my way out the door, though not enough to delete the tweet.

*So they missed me this time. I was lucky. So I'll wag a finger in their faces hoping some Taliban intern manning their Twitter feed doesn't notice and alert middle management, which in turn floats the idea to the Quetta Shura that this is the perfect day to attack the airport and wipe out that obnoxious reporter prick who thinks he can badmouth us and a dozen others. It's far-fetched, grandiose logic bordering on melodramatic delusions of grandeur.*

I reread my tweet a dozen times, then decide to leave it up.

All packed except for my laptop, I scroll through the latest news from here while waiting for my taxi to the airport, trying to ignore the question that's been gnawing at me these last few weeks: *What the fuck do I do now?*

I spent eight months recovering from my injuries and another four getting the Afghanistan bogeyman off my back. Overcoming my loss of vision and returning to where I was hurt was my sole ambition. Now that I've done it, I have no idea what to do next.

*Do I come back to Afghanistan? If so, when?*

I've already started thinking about a return trip in the winter. I've always wanted to do a cold-weather embed in the mountains, though interest in the war wanes when the fighting season slows down.

*What do I do in the meantime?*

I'm technically homeless. My last known address is The Failure Cave. I've left some clothes, my surfboards, and Lucille there. But I can't very well spend the rest of my life living in a converted garage.

*Can I?*

These last four months I felt like I had a purpose. I was doing something that mattered, something at which I was fairly good.

But it didn't make me whole the way I thought it would. I'm still restless and dissatisfied. I don't want to leave. But *USA Today* is tapped out and won't take any more stories.

*I guess I could throw together a couple more clients and keep working through the winter, make a go of living here full time, maybe stay all the way through the next fighting season, then the one after that. I could make this my new home. It makes sense. There's nothing for me in the States except questions to which I don't have any answers. I'm lost there.*

My cell phone buzzes. The taxi is outside the Diana waiting to take me to the airport. I consider waving him off, then shoulder my bags and head out to the gate, wondering whether I'm making the right decision.


The congested streets of Kabul roll by on the other side of my partially rolled down window while I smoke one last cigarette and wonder how anyone here can be happy. In a country mired in decades of war leaving millions of people dead, how can anyone so much as force a smile? Yet they do. Afghans persevere. They throw wedding parties and celebrate the end of Ramadan with food and revelry. They've known unfathomable sadness yet find ways to laugh. They find joy hiding in the small crevices of their terror-filled existence because it's the only way to survive.

*How the fuck can they do that?*

I know the answer to my stupid question. It's evident in every horror I've covered: be it natural disaster or atrocities manufactured by despots.

*They have no other choice.*

If I weren't such a self-pitying sad sack, I would heed their examples and not sit here worrying about my own uncertain future which is infinitely brighter than that of the barefoot, dirt-smeared children playing on the side of the road leading to the airport they'll never visit, where a plane will transport me to a world they'll never know.

I consider my various misfortunes and luck all the way through to ticketing, where I have to slip the agent an extra 100 bucks to get my body armor on the plane.

*It's OK. I'll expense the bribe.*

I'm still contemplating them while stuffing my camera bag into the plane's overhead compartment. I sit down and watch the cavalcade of fellow passengers board the flight to Dubai. Security contractors in cargo pants and tactical shirts with a million pockets (I shouldn't talk—I'm sporting the same gear); Afghan businessmen (i.e., gangsters with suitcases stuffed with cash), UN workers (easily identified because their shoes are always shiny from having rarely touched the Kabul streets) and others heading for the futuristic, Emirate oasis.

*What a bunch of lucky motherfuckers.*

We're all escaping relatively unscathed, even though I'm willing to bet a sizable portion of the people on this flight have had a friend or family member killed over the years.

I've been luckier than most in that sense. I've seen soldiers get hurt, innocents killed, and suffered my own near-death incident. But no one I loved has ever been lost to senseless war. As the plane races down the runway, then its nose tips upward, I concede I really can't complain at all. Only upwardly mobile people of near infinite means compared to those left struggling on the ground would bemoan a fortune as good as mine.

# CHAPTER 38
# NINE MONTHS LATER . . .

JULY, 6, 2012
COMBAT OUTPOST PIRTLE KING, KUNAR PROVINCE, AFGHANISTAN

The helicopter touches down in Pirtle King's small landing zone just before midnight. It's only on the deck for a hot second, just long enough for me to jump off and start sprinting toward the handful of plywood huts on the other side of the base. My camera bag clangs off my back with every stride as the helicopter takes off, its rotor wash swallowing me in a cloud of dust and stinging gravel.

Prior to my arrival here, the flight crew told me there would be no dilly-dallying when we landed at PK. If I wanted to avoid being riddled full of holes courtesy of Taliban snipers, I'd better haul ass once the bird landed.

I labor under the weight of my bags and body armor as I head full bore toward the other side of the outpost. Even in the pitch black, I sorta know where I'm going, though stumble midstride on the loose rocks, nearly tumbling ass-over-ankles before arresting my fall. Something falls off me while catching my step. I pat my pockets for my wallet, cell, and pens.

*All there.*

I grope the top of my baseball hat above the brim. They aren't there. My protective eyeglasses are missing. They must have popped off midstumble.

*You've already lost your eyepro at PK . . . That figures.*

I cooked up the idea of returning to the scene of my injury following my embeds last summer. This assignment for *USA Today* marks the third time I've been back to Afghanistan since getting shot. While planning this trip, I decided to add PK to my list of embeds, even though a part of me surmised there was a small, albeit very real, chance I'd have a psychotic flashback/ breakdown once I got here. I reasoned through my apprehensions about returning that coming back to Pirtle King was somehow cathartic. Coming back would allow me to move on. Memories of what happened during my last embed here are still never far from the forefront of my mind. I replay my injury and the events that followed so often I sometimes feel like I'm not really living in the present. It's something my new girlfriend notices and occasionally mentions, the far-off expression, having to tell me the same thing over and over. She suggests I get a CAT scan. I tell her forget it. It's not my brain that's bothering me. It's what's stored inside that keeps me at arm's length.

I reasoned that my return to PK will allow me to close some psychological loop, perhaps only then escorting my injury into the deeper recesses of memory, at least far enough back that I occasionally focus on the present.

I thought it impossible, but living conditions at PK have actually gotten worse since I was last here. There's a rash of illness going around the base that the guys have dubbed the "PK Fever," a polite descriptor for the bunghole-dilating diarrhea and chills brought on by the unsanitary conditions. Guys afflicted with the PK Fever are out of luck if they need to relieve themselves during the day, however, as the threat of Taliban sniper fire is so great that many of them won't risk running out to the latrine for fear of being shot on the way to, during, or after taking a shit. These days going number two is best saved till after sundown.

That is, if you can hold it.

PK has been built up to better protect its residents, reflecting the growing threat outside its walls. There are now a series of corridors made of eight-foot-high metal baskets filled with rock and dirt reminiscent of World War I trenches. Camouflage netting is draped overhead. When they do venture outside the corridors during the day, the men will often look up at the mountains, take a deep breath, then dash toward the barracks on the other side of the out-post a few dozen yards away hoping to not get shot.

Those soldiers and goofball reporters venturing outside PK's corridors are required to wear their body armor and helmets while making the dash, a trade-off considering the armor might keep you alive if hit, though increases your chances of getting shot by slowing your gait. It's a toss-up really.

Despite these precautions prompted by legitimate concerns, Company Commander Capt. Erik Norman tells me it's been pretty quiet these last few weeks. Not so much as a single shot fired on PK, says the almost comedically tall and lanky commanding officer, whose security assessment barely registers in my ears when the first crack of gunfire whizzes across the combat outpost. Several shots follow in quick succession before a barrage of rocket-propelled grenades land inside the outpost and just outside the walls.

The explosions send a handful of soldiers tumbling to the ground. They quickly recover their footing and return fire into the nearby mountains hoping to at least hit one of the unseen assailants up there.

I grab my video camera and start rolling on a couple of soldiers firing mortars. They're wearing T-shirts and shorts. The AK-47 rounds hiss, then snap. The gunmen in the mountains are zeroing in on a cluster of guys in the open.

I pull back and look for the captain, who is conferring with his men. One of them was in the middle of getting an IV for severe fluid loss caused by the PK Fever when the attack started, a ragged track mark on his forearm trickles blood from where he pulled out the needle. I still can't handle needles. Looking at his forearm makes me want to vomit.

I flash to my injury: the bandages wrapping my caved-in face and pulver-ized eye; the ringing in my head. Uncertainty and fear.

*Stop it!*

I tell myself to focus on the fight with my cameras—the view through my lenses will create enough space between me and reality to remain sane and composed.

*Do your job!*

I turn off my video camera, assess the situation.

*If you get hurt here again . . .*

During a brief lull in the shooting, Captain Norman sidles up to me and says with a smirk: "Someone knows you're back."

I cock my head and laugh.

"Ha!"

## THE END

# ACKNOWLEDGMENTS

It's been a winding, ass-cracking, sometimes nauseating journey from when I first conceived *Blindsided by the Taliban* to publication of the bundle of pages and glue (or tablet version) in front of you.

Every author to whom I spoke about publishing my first book said I should be prepared for loads of rejection. In hindsight, I'm glad I didn't ask for clarification regarding how many "no thanks" constitutes "loads," lest I would have probably given up after the first one hundred form-letter "FU's" from agents and editors.

So I'd like to thank Skyhorse Publishing for their faith in my story when others thought I was either A) making it up, or B) not enough of a household name to warrant a book-length recounting of a most unusual story told with explicit, embarrassing detail and swearing, i.e., how I talk in real life.

Fortunately for me, the folks at Skyhorse paired me with editor Mike Campbell, who helped me trim the unsightly fat in places and beef up the story in others to make *Blindsided by the Taliban* the best book it can be. When we met for the first time Mike told me: "Your book is the kind people are either going to love or hate." Seeing as how that's exactly the kind of book I set out to write, I couldn't have asked for a better person to help me despite him being young enough to be my prom baby.

However, the most arduous part of the journey to the promise land of publication came before finding the right home for *Blindsided by the Taliban*. It was then that I received loads of much-needed advice and encouragement from those who sometimes had more faith in my story than I did.

Janet Steen, a fellow Pittsburgher, provided keen insights and suggestions that proved invaluable, as did high school friend and former underage boozing cohort Maryll Botula.

Fellow journalist Matt Stroud not only made excellent suggestions, but he was also good enough to give my beloved motorcycle a home while I traipsed around the world working on the book and committing the occasional act of journalism.

Rounding out my hometown brain trust was Annie Siebert, who offered to pour over the text with her sharp copy editor's eye because she said she was hooked after reading the first chapter. That meant a lot to me at a time when I was near drowning in doubt.

When I moved to Istanbul a few years ago to revise my exceptionally rough first draft, I met Defne Tabori, who asked to read said flawed manuscript in a single evening. Her enthusiasm for *Blindsided by the Taliban* and willingness to champion it far and wide kept me emotionally afloat when no one in the book business was singing similar praises.

Author Angie McCormick Ricketts did likewise, telling me time and again how much she enjoyed the story and that eventually others would too.

I must also give special thanks to Amber Robinson, an Army veteran who appears in the story, albeit too briefly, for helping me set the proper tone in the first few pages. Your notes were crucial, Sgt. Rob.

I have what's best described as a love-hate relationship with Miami, where I lived for many years, though didn't always know why. But I'm glad I stuck around because otherwise I wouldn't have had the pleasure of befriending Bruce Bernstein, who provided me with shelter during the dark times and let me store bikes, surfboards, and other assorted relics of my life at his house.

Special thanks to Catharine Skipp, who let me write some of my book at a desk she snagged from the *Washington Post*'s Miami bureau that had made its way from DC decades earlier and once belonged to legendary editor Ben Bradlee. When I was writing, I would occasionally kick my feet up on that hulking mass of wooden history and feel like the king of storytelling and journalism, neither of which I am in real life, though it was fun to pretend.

A handful of long-time Afghanistan reporters also provided helpful suggestions and frank criticism which I hated at first, though later realized were right on the mark. Tom Peter, Heath Druzin and Martin Kuz, all residents of Soft Target Number 7 in Kabul, thank you.

Another excellent Afghanistan reporter, Jason Motlagh, helped with the book's original title, which I believe captures the story's irreverence and dark humor. It's located on the back cover and is the preferred hashtag for when you're cracking wise on social media about my clumsy prose and deplorable behavior.

Final thanks goes to my wife Nina, who read my book before we got together and somehow wasn't frightened away, and our daughter Francesca, who's darling smile reminded me amid the onslaught of rejections that most things are way more important than the world of publishing.

I'd also like to take this time to apologize to all those I hurt along the way. I won't humiliate you by singling you out. Besides, the list alone might be longer than the book. I wasn't always nice or considerate leading up to and after my injury. I could make a bunch of lame excuses, but I won't. I was a dick, plain and simple.

Extra special apologies to my folks and family. I'm aware you might be mad at me after reading this.